Paolo Peti

Spaghetti *my love*

More than 100 delicious,
simple recipes for spaghetti,
bucatini and linguine

GIUNTI

Editor
Roberto De Meo

Coordinator
David Pacifici

Art direction
Constanza Di Gregorio

Page layout and cover design
Adria Villa

Revision
Simona Pelagotti

Photographs:
by R. Germogli except the following:
Archivio Giunti: foto M. Favi, p.12, p.17, p.18, p.19, p.20, p.21, p.22, p.23;
G. Petronio, pp. 24-25, p.79, p.139.
©Stockfood/Olycom, p.3, p.5, p.17.

www.giunti.it

Via Bolognese 165 - 50139 Firenze - Italia
Via Dante 4 - 20121 Milano - Italia
First edition: february 2009

Reprint	Year
5 4 3 2 1 0	2013 2012 2011 2010 2009

Printed by Giunti Industrie Grafiche S.p.A. – Prato (Italy)

Contents

Preface

Pasta is the emblem of Italian cuisine. Therefore it is only natural that the majority of Italian cookbooks focus on the subject. Yet often we come across recipes with long and complex cooking procedures that ultimately do not work.
This nimble and complete book is dedicated exclusively to pasta seen as the essence of the soul: dry long pasta to be more specific. It is a book about spaghetti, linguine and bucatini, among others.
It is a comprehensive, precise and easy to understand manual.

The first section of the book in particular is dedicated to the history of pasta, its characteristics and the way to cook it. It represents the most complete discussion on pasta found in any other cookbook out there. Finally, its convenient pocket size and its easy and quick recipes make it the prefect companion for those who are always searching for an unlimited source of appetizing recipes.

Paolo Petroni

Dry Pasta

The origins of pasta

The term "pasta" encompasses so much on its own, that it is almost impossible to talk about its origins. If for "pasta" we mean any type of dough made with flour and water, steamed or boiled and seasoned with different sauces made out of fat, cheese, meat, or fish, we have then decoded the mystery behind Eastern and Mediterranean culinary history.

"Gnocchi" are the original pasta. To be more precise, these were pasta balls or small buns (called *laganon*, or *itryah*) made with water, oats or spelt, that were baked on a hot stone, cut in pieces and boiled in water; a very similar preparation of today's "testaroli della Lunigiana".

That is why we should focus solely on dry pasta made from durum wheat (semolina). It is easier to talk about "vermicelli" (the oldest term applied to pasta, year 1287; and still used in Campania and Calabria) and about "spaghetti" (a term applied since 1836).

The Sicilian term for pasta and one of the oldest is "maccheroni" (*maccarruni*), which is in itself very generic and used to identify all types of pasta, not only spaghetti. In Northern and Central Italy macaroni are short, thick hollow pasta (like rigatoni, sedani etc.). In Southern Italy, especially in Naples, they are called spaghetti, linguine, ziti, bucatini, or perciatelli. In Sicily and in Calabria there is a type of home made pasta made with "il ferretto" (a stick used to roll

the pasta into a hollow tube). And very popular are also "maccheroni alla chitarra" (*guitar macaroni*) from Abruzzo which are square-shaped spaghetti made with eggs and durum wheat flour.
There are numerous theories about the origin of spaghetti (almost always based on unevidenced assumptions). The three most successful are the following:

Arab-Sicilian origin

In the 1154 "Libro per chi si diletta di girare il Mondo" (*The Book for those who enjoy travelling around the World*), also called "Il Libro di Ruggero" (*Ruggero's Book*), dedicated to Ruggero II of Sicily also named "Il Normanno" (*The Norman*), Arab author Al Idrisi says that «a powerful person from Termini Imerese had many farms and flour mills where such a large quantity of "vermicelli" was made that it could supply not only the Calabria Region, but also other Muslim and Christian territories». It is assumed then that the pasta was dry and made to last long voyages.

The word vermicelli comes from the Arabic *itriya*. To this day the term *tria* is used in Syracuse (spaghettini sottili - *thin small spaghetti*), in Basilicata (lunghi spaghetti - *long spaghetti*) and in Puglia (tagliatelle di farina di grano duro e acqua - *durum wheat flour noodles with water*).

Ligurian origins

A notary contract written for a first draft testament in 1279 Genova explains that among many inventions, there was «una bariscella plena de macaronis» (*a barrel full of macaroni*). It is not clear exactly what these "macaronis" were, however, since they were left as inheritance, it is implied that they were dry preserved pasta. It is true that Genova, having a very active port, must have imported semolina and other culinary traditions from Sicily, or directly from Arabic Countries.

The mild and ventilate climate in Liguria has always been perfect to dehydrate pasta. That is why, according to documents dating as far as

1244, Liguria has been denominated the homeland of the dried pasta. In 1574 the "Corporazione dei Pastai" called The Fidelari, (*the Pasta Makers Corporation*) was created in Genova. At the same time in 1794 Savona was celebrated for the most antique Italian pasta store.

Chinese origins

It is said that Marco Polo, brought back spaghetti from his trips to China and that he wrote about it in his journals. This theory is not all true.

Chinese are experts in the craft of hand made pasta, but they utilize soy and rice flour, which cannot be preserved. In any case, in 1295 when Marco Polo returned from his journeys, dry pasta and spaghetti were already widely known.

Pasta meets tomato

Whatever the origin of spaghetti, it is certain that since the early 1300's, it was mostly known in Northeast Italy. It wasn't until the 1500's that it became common all over Italy, except for Naples where, believe it or not, pasta was considered a luxury. The first pasta factory was build in Torre Annunziata in 1840.

Neapolitans were known as "mangiafoglia" (*leaf eaters*), because they enjoyed eating vegetables and broccoli soup, while Sicilians were called "mangiamaccheroni" (*macaroni eaters*).

For centuries pasta was cooked in soup or milk and seasoned with butter, lard, cheese and spices and sometimes mixed with sweets like sugar and cinnamon. It is understandable to think that the real success of pasta came with the invention of tomato sauce (originally from America), in the beginning of the 17th century. The first book about tomato sauce (with no mention of pasta) was "Scalco alla moderna" by Antonio Latini, published in Naples in 1694. It contained the first sauce recipe "Salsa di pomodoro alla spagnuola" (*Spanish tomato sauce*), prepared with onion, thyme, pepper, salt, oil and vinegar.

Much later, in 1773, the famous cookbook "Il cuoco galante" (*The Gallant Cook*), by Vincenzo Corrado, featured different types of tomato

and sauce recipes, but still with no indication of macaroni.
The first author to unite tomatoes with pasta was Antonio Nebbia, in his 1779 book "Cuoco maceratese" (*The Chef from Macerata*). Another trace was found in 1807 in an anonymous recipe book, but it is not until 1839 with the book "La cucina teorico-pratica" (*Theoric and practical Cooking*), published by Ippolito Cavalcanti, the Duke of Buonvicino, that we will find the first recipe to do the union "vermicelli co' lo pomodoro" (*spaghetti with tomato sauce*).

Therefore, without a doubt, pasta is a modern food. Its origin is pretty much "proletarian". Actually it was never found in old cooking recipes of royal court chefs or in aristocratic banquets.

Industrial dry pasta

Hand-made pasta was originally made in Sicily, Calabria and Puglia. The pasta industry on the other hand has its origins in the Ligurian Riviera during the early 1800's (in 1812 there were around 148 pasta factories in Imperia and Savona). The dry and ventilated climate of the region is perfect for dehydrating pasta.

In 1840 a new business, the Neapolitan Pasta Masters, started to grow rapidly thanks to the success of pasta "all'uso di Genova" (*the Genova way*). At the beginning of the 19th Century, Naples (specifically Gragnano, Torre Annunziata e Torre del Greco) became the Worldwide Capital of pasta, even if, during the same period, the Pasta Masters of Abruzzo created culinary products of equal or greater quality.
Today's modern pasta factories no longer need this specific, ventilated climate. Therefore, pasta can be produced almost anywhere; actually, today's technology has actually improved the quality and the shelf life of pasta. The science of nourishment has supported the value of this culinary product by including it in the Mediterranean diet which has had worldwide acclaim.

The quality of pasta

Dry pasta is exclusively made with durum wheat flour, also called semolina, that is kneaded with water. Since the procedure to make the dough is so complex, today the production is only industrial.
Unfortunately, today's laws allow for pasta to be made with different types of flour that are not as good as semolina. Read the labels on packages carefully and trust only the most famous pasta makers.
Dry pasta can also be made with eggs (tagliatelle, fettuccine, pappardelle, lasagna noodles, etc.). But keep in mind, that the law requires only 4 eggs (including dehydrated, powder eggs) per 1 kilo of flour.

The quality of pasta varies according to the brand and to the following factors:

- The variety of semolina used
- The grain and dimension of the flour
- The quality of water used for kneading
- The quantity and temperature of the water used
- The materials applied during the procedure (normally it is Teflon®, but the best is bronze because it gives a wrinkly and light yellow aspect)
- The dehydration process (traditionally it was at a low temperature [110-120 °F] with a duration of 20 to 40 hours; today it is done at a higher temperature [sometimes over 75 °F] with a duration of 8 to 10 hours; the most common is at a high temperature with a duration of only 4 hours).

Good pasta must be slightly wrinkled, but shiny with a yellow/gold color. Pasta that has a white, or amber color is not that good. While cooking, the water must remain pretty clear; milky water is a clear sign of a low quality pasta.
Trust the most expensive and well known brands and then just follow your palate to make the final decision.

The many shapes of long pasta

Even if today there are exaggerated amounts of pasta shapes (there are hundreds and always new ones are coming out), it is good to know that the shape of pasta is not only an aesthetic matter, but that it is also about substance. Various formats have different tastes, different cooking times and are meant to be seasoned with different sauces.

Unfortunately, every brand has its own name of pasta, so the confusion can be enormous. Fortunately though, on every package there is the cooking time so from that you can understand what type of spaghetti it is; the following is a guide to understand the major and most common formats of long pasta.

NAMES	COOKING MINUTES	MAJOR USES
Capellini	3-4	Perfect for butter and grated parmigiano, caprese sauce, tomato sauce, in soup
Spaghettini or vermicellini	5-6	It is the standard Neapolitan size for long pasta; ideal for seafood sauces, vegetables and fresh tomato sauces and "puttanesca"
Spaghetti or vermicelli	7-8	It is the most classic format. Perfect with any type of sauce, la "pummarola" and "carbonara"
Spaghettoni or vermicelloni	10-12	Perfect for meat sauces, with pancetta, "amatriciana"
Linguine or bavettine (Born in Liguria)	7-8	Perfect for pesto, seafood sauces, vegetables and with butter and grated cheese
Trenette	8-10	Similar to linguine but a little larger with square edge. In Liguria you can also find "trenette avvantaggiate" which are darker because they are made with whole wheat flour
Perciatellini or foratini	8-10	They are spaghetti with a small hole; perfect for meat sauces, Neapolitan sauce, amatriciana and also with butter and grated cheese
Bucatini (Roman term) or Perciatelli (Neapolitan term)	11-12	Ideal for "amatriciana", Neapolitan sauce, broccoli, swordfish sauce
Ziti or zite	10-12	Baked with smoked cheeses, eggplant, Neapolitan meat sauce, Sicilian sauce
Fusilli	15-17	Tomato sauce, "pomarola", Neapolitan ragù

How to cook pasta

The container

Use a good quality pot with a thick bottom to guarantee equal and consistent heat.
If you prefer big portions, I would suggest a 7 liter, 25 cm tall pot for 4 people.
I do not advise to use a pot with separate pasta draining pan insert. It delays the cooking time, reduces space for the pasta, makes noise and does not make the drainage any easier.

Water and salt

Boil 1 liter (1 quart/4 cups) of water for every 3 ounces of pasta. When the water starts to boil, add 1 full teaspoon of coarse salt per person.

Cooking procedure

After a few minutes, add the pasta to the salted boiling water.
Raise the heat and stir the pasta with a big wooden fork to ensure that all the pasta is soaked in the water.
When the pasta is "al dente", drain and pour into a warm bowl.

The dressing

Pour the sauce over the pasta and toss.
If you need to sauté the pasta with the sauce, drain the pasta a minute earlier and finish cooking with the sauce.

For an easy, comfortable and safe cooking procedure of pasta, the author of this book has created a perfect and ideal spaghetti pot named ARCA© (for more information, please visit the website www.brandani.it).

1

POUR THE WATER TO THE DESIRED LEVEL: 1 LEVEL PER PERSON

2

ADD SALT WITH THE APPROPRIATE MEASURE SPOON

3

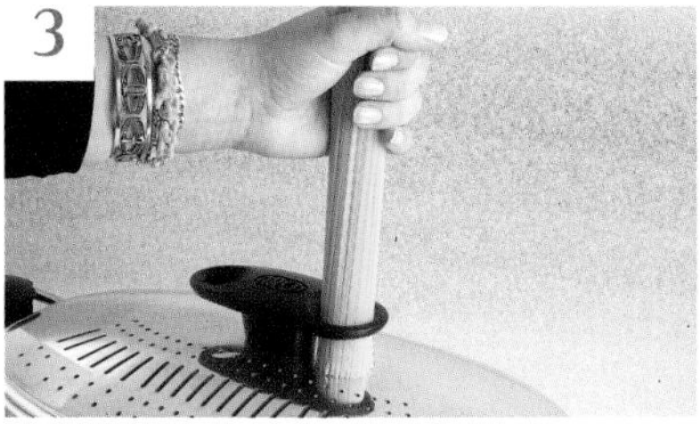

MEASURE THE PASTA: SMALL HOLE FOR 1 PERSON, BIG HOLE FOR 2 PEOPLE

4

ADD THE PASTA: IT WILL BE TOTALLY SUBMERGED IN THE BOILING WATER RIGHT AWAY

5

TASTE WITH THE APPROPRIATE ACCESSORY

6

DRAIN THE PASTA DIRECTLY WITH ITS LID

MEASURING WITH SPOONS AND CUPS

	METRIC
1 teaspoon	
water, oil, etc.	4-5 ml
flour, salt, sugar (leveled)	4-5 g
flour, salt, sugar (full)	8-10 g
1 tablespoon = 3 teaspoons	
water, oil, etc.	12-15 ml
flour, salt, sugar (leveled)	12-15 g
flour, salt, sugar (full)	20-25 g
rice (full)	15-20 g
grated cheese	10-15 g
butter	15-20 g
1 cup = 16 tablespoons	
water, oil, etc.	230-250 ml
flour	120-140 g
sugar, rice	180-210 g
1 glass	
water	150-200 ml
wine	120-140 ml
liquor (small glass)	40-60 ml

Basic Sauces of Italian cuisine

RAGÙ BOLOGNESE

Bologness sauce

Serves 6

- 5 ounces ground beef
- 5 ounces ground pork
- 3 ounces pancetta, minced
- 1 carrot, peeled and diced
- 1 stalk celery, diced
- 1 onion, diced
- 8 ounces peeled ripe tomatoes, seeds removed, chopped
- 1 tablespoon tomato paste
- 3 tablespoons butter
- 1/2 cup red wine
- 1/2 cup heavy cream (optional)
- olive oil
- salt and pepper

1. In a deep skillet, warm the butter with 3 tablespoons of olive oil. Add the pancetta, onion, carrot and celery and sauté over low heat for about 1 minutes.

2. When the vegetables starts to brown, add the pork and beef. Season with salt and pepper and cook, stirring for a couple of minutes. Deglaze with the wine and cook until it evaporates.

3. Add the peeled tomatoes and continue to cook, covered for 30 minutes. At this point, stir in the tomato paste diluted in 1/2 cup of warm water or stock. Continue to cook over low heat, covered for about 1 hour. At the end, before removing from the heat, add the heavy cream and cook until it starts to reduce.

Ragù napoletano o "Rraù del guardaporta"

Neapolitan meat sauce or "Doorkeeper's Ragù"

Serves 6

18

- 3 1/2 pounds beef in one piece
- 2 ounces prosciutto crudo
- 4 ounces pancetta
- 2 large onions
- 2 cloves garlic
- 1/2 cup dry red wine
- 2 tablespoons tomato paste
- 14 ounces peeled ripe tomatoes, seeds removed and chopped
- olive oil
- salt and freshly ground pepper

1. Chop the prosciutto into strips and roll it in pepper. Lard the beef with the prosciutto and set aside. In a skillet over medium heat, warm the olive oil. Add the pancetta, onion and garlic and sauté until soft. Add the meat and brown on all sides. Cover and cook slowly, turning occasionally.
2. When the onion starts to brown, deglaze with half the wine and cook until it starts to evaporate. Add the remaining wine and cook slowly, covered, for about 1 hour, or until it starts to become thick.
3. At this point, add the tomatoes and the tomato paste dissolved in enough boiling water to cover the beef. Season with salt and bring to a boil. Lower the heat and simmer for 3 hours.
4. Remove the meat from the skillet and keep warm. Cook the sauce for another hour, or until reduced by half. Slice the meat and serve with the sauce.

SUGO DI CARNE TOSCANO

Tuscan meat sauce

Serves 6

- 14 ounces beef (rump steak, brisket), sliced
- 1 pound peeled ripe tomatoes, seeds removed and chopped
- 2 cups combined chopped celery, onion and carrot
- 6 tablespoons olive oil
- salt and freshly ground pepper

1. In a skillet over medium heat, warm the olive oil. Add the parsley, celery, onion and carrot and cook for 20 minutes. Add the slices of meat and brown on both sides.
2. Remove the meat from the skillet and chop finely. Return to the skillet and add the tomatoes. Season with salt and pepper and cook slowly, covered, for about 1 hour.

RAGÙ PUGLIESE O "DEL MACELLAIO"

Apulian meat sauce or "Butcher's Ragù"

Serves 8

- 5 ounces beef, cubed
- 5 ounces pork, cubed
- 5 ounces lamb, cubed
- 4 ounces pancetta, diced
- 9 ounces peeled ripe tomatoes, seeds removed and chopped
- 1 tablespoon tomato paste
- 1 onion, chopped
- 2 cloves garlic, minced
- 1/2 cup dry white wine
- minced chili pepper to taste
- 6 tablespoons olive oil
- salt

1. In a deep skillet, warm the olive oil. Add the onion, garlic and chili pepper and cook until they start to brown.

2. Add the pancetta and cook until browned. Deglaze with half the wine and cook until it starts to evaporate. Add the lamb, beef and pork, deglaze with the remaining wine and cook until it starts to evaporate.

3. Add the tomatoes and the tomato paste, season with salt and pepper and cook over low heat, covered, for about 2 hours, adding hot water if it starts to dry.

Add chopped chicken or sausage the last 30 minutes of the cooking time if desired.

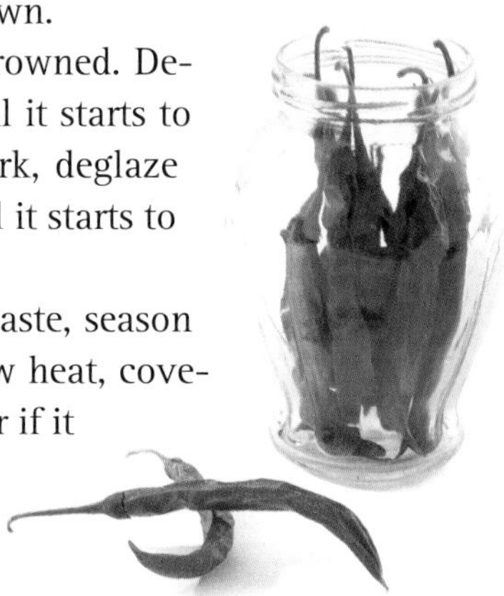

Ragù di rigaglie

Giblets sauce

Serves 6

- 9 ounces chicken innards (liver, heart, gizzard)
- 9 ounces peeled ripe tomatoes, seeds removed and chopped
- 1 medium onion
- 2 sage leaves
- 1/2 cup wine
- 2 tablespoons butter
- 3 tablespoons olive oil
- salt and freshly ground pepper

1. Trim and chop the chicken innards. In a skillet over medium heat, melt the butter with the oil. Add the onion and sage and sauté until soft.

2. Add the tripe, cook for about 2 minutes and deglaze with the wine. When it begins to evaporate, add the tomatoes, season with salt and pepper and cook until it thickens.

3. At this point, add the liver and heart. Cook for another 10 minutes and remove from the heat.

Ragù bianco

White meat sauce

Serves 6

- 6 ounces veal
- 5 ounces pork
- 4 ounces chicken breast
- 1 small onion, chopped
- 1 small carrot, peeled and diced
- rosemary
- ½ cup white wine
- stock
- 4 tablespoons olive oil
- salt and freshly ground pepper

1. In a skillet, warm the olive oil. Add the carrot, onion and rosemary.
2. When the onion starts to soften, add the meat. Deglaze with the wine and cook until it evaporates.
3. Remove the meat from the skillet and chop finely. Return to the skillet and season with salt and pepper. Cook for another 30 minutes, adding stock gradually.
4. Cook until the sauce starts to thicken. The sauce should be homogenous and creamy enough to serve over fettuccine or tagliatelle (noodles).

Salsa di funghi

Mushroom sauce

Serves 6

- 10 ounces fresh porcini mushrooms
- 10 ounces peeled ripe tomatoes, seeds removed, chopped
- 2 cloves garlic
- chopped mint or parsley
- 6 tablespoons olive oil
- salt and freshly ground pepper

1. Wash and peel the mushrooms and chop. In a skillet over medium heat, warm the olive oil. Add the garlic and herbs and when they start to brown, add the mushrooms.
2. Season with salt and pepper and cook, stirring with a wooden spoon, until the liquid starts to evaporate. Add the tomatoes (if you want to make a white sauce, add vegetable stock instead) and continue to cook for 20 minutes.

Salsa di pomodoro o "Pummarola"

Traditional tomato sauce

Serves 8

- 2 pounds peeled ripe tomatoes, seeds removed and chopped
- 1 medium onion, finely chopped
- 1 stalk celery, chopped
- 2 carrots, peeled and diced
- 6 basil leaves, shredded
- 8 tablespoons olive oil
- chopped parsley
- salt

1. In a large skillet, combine the olive oil with the tomatoes, onion, celery, carrot, basil and parsley.
2. Season with salt and place over medium heat. Cook for about 1 hour.
3. Set aside to cool and strain into a food mill.
4. Return the strained sauce to the stove and cook to the desired consistency.

SUGO FINTO O "SCAPPATO" O "DI POMODORO"

Traditional tomato sauce

Serves 4

- 1 pound peeled tomatoes, seeds removed, chopped
- 1 medium onion, finely chopped
- 2 medium carrots, peeled and diced
- 2 stalks celery, diced
- chopped parsley
- 1/2 cup red wine
- olive oil
- salt and freshly ground pepper

1. In a skillet over medium heat, warm 6 tablespoons of olive oil. Add the carrot, onion and celery and sauté.
2. When the vegetables are soft, add the parsley and deglaze with the wine. Cook over low heat until the wine starts to evaporate.
3. Add the tomatoes, season with salt and pepper and cook for about 1 hour, stirring occasionally. The sauce should be thick and flavorful.

Recipes

Identifying the recipes

The recipes identified with a green-colored title are based on a vegetables or cheese, the ones in blue contain fish and seafood, and the red ones are based on meat or meat products.
For quick and complete access to the recipes in the book, consult the ingredient index at the end. Consider also that pasta makers don't use the same names to describe the same types of long pasta. To understand the type of pasta that you have in front of you, you must refer exclusively to the chart on page 13.

Spaghetti con Acciughe sotto sale

Spaghetti with anchovies

Serves 4

- 12 ounces thick spaghetti or bucatini
- 4 tablespoons dried bread crumbs
- 4 anchovy fillets packed in salt, rinsed
- 2 cloves garlic
- Olive oil
- salt and freshly ground pepper

1 In a skillet, warm 8 tablespoons of olive oil. Chop the anchovies and add to the skillet. Add the anchovies and cook over low heat, stirring, until they dissolve.

2 In a separate skillet, warm 2 tablespoons of olive oil. Add the bread crumbs and toast.

3 Cook the pasta in salted boiling water until al dente. Drain and add to the skillet with the anchovies. Serve sprinkled with the toasted bread crumbs and a grinding of pepper. (Sprinkle with chopped parsley if desired).

Spaghetti alle Acciughe fresche

Spaghetti with fresh anchovies

Serves 4

- 12 ounces spaghetti or linguine
- 14 ounces fresh anchovies
- 10 ounces peeled ripe tomatoes, seeds removed
- 1 clove garlic, minced
- chopped parsley
- minced chili pepper to taste
- 1/4 cup white wine
- olive oil
- salt

1 Fillet the anchovies, removing the heads and tails.

2 In a skillet, warm 6 tablespoons of olive oil. Add the garlic, parsley and chili pepper, and sauté for a couple of minutes. Deglaze with the wine, and cook until it evaporates.

3 Add the tomatoes, season with salt, and cook for 10 minutes, stirring occasionally.

4 Add the anchovies, and cook for another 5 minutes.

5 Cook the pasta in salted boiling water until al dente. Drain, and add to the anchovy sauce. Toss over high heat, and serve.

Spaghetti *Aglio e olio*

Spaghetti with oil and garlic

Serves 4

- 12 ounces spaghetti or linguine
- 2 large cloves garlic, sliced
- minced chili pepper to taste
- chopped parsley
- olive oil
- salt and freshly ground pepper
- grated pecorino (optional)

1 In a large skillet, warm 6 tablespoons of olive oil. Add the garlic and the chili pepper and sauté until the garlic starts to brown.

2 Cook the pasta in salted boiling water. Drain and add to the skillet with the garlic.

3 Sprinkle with parsley and pepper and toss. Serve with pecorino on the side.

Spaghetti alla chitarra al ragù di Agnello

Chitarra spaghetti with lamb sauce

Serves 4

- 14 ounces chitarra spaghetti (square spaghetti typical of the Abruzzi)
- 10 ounces lamb, diced
- 2 red or yellow bell peppers, seeds and inner white ribbing removed, diced
- 10 ounces (1 1/4 cups) peeled ripe tomatoes, seeds removed, chopped
- 2 cloves garlic, minced
- 1/2 cup white wine
- 1 bay leaf
- minced chili pepper to taste
- flour
- olive oil
- salt

1 In a skillet, warm 6 tablespoons of olive oil. Add the garlic, chili pepper and bay leaf and sauté. Dredge the lamb in flour and add to the skillet.

2 Cook until the lamb browns on all sides. Deglaze with half the wine and cook until it evaporates. Add the remaining wine and cook until it starts to evaporate.

3 Add the tomatoes and bell peppers, season with salt and pepper and cook over low heat for about 1 hour, or until the lamb is very tender.

4 Cook the pasta in salted boiling water until al dente. Drain and serve with the lamb sauce.

Bucatini all' Amatriciana

Bucatini with pancetta and tomatoes

Serves 4

- 12 ounces bucatini or thick spaghetti
- 14 ounces peeled ripe tomatoes, seeds removed, chopped
- 4 ounces pancetta or guanciale (pig's cheek)
- minced chili pepper to taste
- olive oil
- salt and pepper
- grated pecorino Romano

1 Finely chop the pancetta and sauté in a skillet with 3 tablespoons of olive oil.

2 When it starts to brown, add the tomatoes. Season with salt and pepper, add the chili pepper and cook over high heat for about 10 minutes.

3 Cook the pasta in salted boiling water until al dente. Drain and add to the sauce.

4 Add some pecorino and toss. Serve with additional pecorino on the side.

Spaghetti all'Aragosta

Spaghetti with lobster

Serves 4

- 12 ounces spaghetti
- 1 lobster, about 1 pound
- 4 peeled ripe tomatoes, seeds removed, chopped
- 2 sun-dried tomatoes, chopped
- 1 clove garlic
- chopped parsley
- minced chili pepper to taste
- ½ cup dry white wine
- olive oil
- salt

1 Chop the lobster and cook in a skillet with 8 tablespoons of olive oil. Add the garlic, parsley, chili pepper and sun-dried tomatoes.

2 Deglaze with the wine and cook until it starts to evaporate.

3 Add the ripe tomatoes, season with salt and pepper and cook, stirring occasionally, for about 20 minutes.

4 Cook the pasta in salted boiling water until al dente. Drain and add to the lobster sauce. Sprinkle with parsley, toss and serve.

Spaghetti all'Arancia

Spaghetti with orange sauce

Serves 4

- 12 ounces spaghetti or linguine
- 1 large orange
- 4 anchovy fillets packed in oil or salt, rinsed
- 1 clove garlic, minced
- chopped parsley
- olive oil
- salt and pepper

1 Peel the orange, removing the white pith. Cut into sections, reserving the juice.

2 In a skillet, warm 6 tablespoons of olive oil. Add the garlic and the anchovies. Cook, stirring, until the anchovies dissolve.

3 Add the orange and orange juice, and season with pepper. Cook for about 10 minutes. If necessary, add some extra orange juice or a bit of wine.

4 Cook the pasta in salted boiling water until al dente. Drain the pasta, and add the orange sauce. Add chopped parsley, and toss. Grated cheese is optional.

Linguine agli Asparagi

Linguine with asparagus

Serves 4

- 12 ounces linguine
- 1 ½ pounds thin asparagus
- 1 cup ricotta
- milk
- salt and freshly ground pepper
- olive oil
- grated Parmigiano

1 Trim and peel the rough bottom part of the asparagus spears. Cook in salted boiling water, drain and cut into small pieces.

2 In a skillet, warm 4 tablespoons of olive oil. Add the asparagus and sauté briefly. Stir in the ricotta and season with salt and pepper.

3 Cook the linguine in salted boiling water. Drain and add to the asparagus.

4 Pour in a bit of milk and toss. Serve sprinkled with the Parmigiano.

Linguine all'Astice

Linguine with small lobster

Serves 4

- 12 ounces linguine
- 2 small lobsters (or 4 jumbo shrimp)
- 4 peeled and seeded ripe tomatoes, chopped
- 2 cloves garlic, sliced
- ½ cup white wine
- 3 tablespoons Brandy or Cognac
- minced chili pepper to taste
- olive oil
- salt

1 In a skillet, warm 6 tablespoons of olive oil and add the lobster, garlic and chili pepper.

2 Season with salt and sauté for about 5 minutes, stirring. Deglaze with the Brandy and cook until it evaporates. Add the wine and cook until it reduces.

3 Add the tomatoes and cook for about 10 minutes.

4 Cook the pasta in salted boiling water until al dente. Drain and add to the lobster sauce. Finish cooking with a bit of water or stock and 2 tablespoons of olive oil.

5 Serve the pasta with the lobster sauce on top.

Spaghetti alla Boscaiola

Spaghetti "woodman's" style

Serves 4

- 12 ounces spaghetti or linguine
- 10 ounces porcini or assorted mushrooms
- 1 clove garlic
- chopped parsley
- olive oil
- salt and freshly ground pepper

1 Peel and quickly wash the mushrooms under cold running water. Thinly slice.

2 In a pan, warm 6 tablespoons of olive oil. Add the parsley and garlic.

3 When they start to brown, add the mushrooms, pour in a bit of water or stock and cook for about 10 minutes. Add chopped parsley at the end.

4 Cook the pasta in salted boiling water until al dente. Drain and add to the mushrooms.

5 Add a grinding of fresh pepper, toss and serve.

Spaghetti alla Bottarga

Spaghetti with bottarga

Serves 4

- 12 ounces spaghetti or linguine
- 2 ounces bottarga (salted mullet or tuna roe)
- 1 clove garlic
- olive oil
- salt and freshly ground white pepper

1 In a skillet, sauté the whole garlic in 6 tablespoons of olive oil until brown. Remove the garlic from the skillet and remove from the heat.

2 Grate half of the bottarga into the skillet, season with salt and stir.

3 Cook the pasta in salted boiling water until al dente. Drain and add to the bottarga. Return to low heat and cook shortly, adding a bit of water and a drizzle of olive oil.

4 Transfer to a platter and serve with a grinding of white pepper. Grate the remaining bottarga on top.

Spaghetti con i Broccoli

Spaghetti with broccoli

Serves 4

- 12 ounces spaghetti or bucatini
- 1 pound broccoli
- 4 anchovies packed in salt
- 1 clove garlic, minced
- olive oil
- salt and freshly ground pepper
- grated pecorino

1 Separate the broccoli stems and the florets and cut into pieces. Cook in salted boiling water for about 5 minutes. Remove the broccoli and set aside. Add the pasta to the boiling water and cook until al dente.

2 Meanwhile, in a skillet warm 6 tablespoons of olive oil. Add the garlic and the anchovies.

3 Stir until the anchovies dissolve and add the broccoli. Cook, adding a tablespoon of the boiling water from the pasta (add some saffron at this time if desired).

4 Drain the pasta and add to the broccoli. Toss well and serve finished with a grinding of pepper and sprinkle with the grated cheese.

Bucatini con Broccoletti uvetta e pinoli

Bucatini with broccoli, raisins, pine nuts

Serves 4

- 12 ounces bucatini or spaghetti
- 1 pound broccoli
- 1/4 cup pine nuts
- 1/4 cup raisins, soaked in warm water
- 2 cloves garlic, minced
- minced chili pepper to taste
- olive oil
- salt
- grated pecorino

1 Trim the broccoli, dividing the stems from the florets and cut into small pieces. Cook in salted boiling water for about 5 minutes. Remove the broccoli from the boiling water and set aside. Add the pasta to the boiling water and cook until al dente.

2 Meanwhile, in a deep skillet, warm 6 tablespoons of olive oil. Add the garlic, pine nuts and raisins.

3 When the garlic starts to brown, add the broccoli and chili pepper. Stir and cook for about 10 minutes.

4 Drain the pasta and add to the broccoli. Toss and serve with the pecorino on the side.

Spaghetti Cacio e pepe

Spaghetti "cheese and pepper"

Serves 4

- 12 ounces spaghetti
- 4 ounces grated pecorino Romano
- freshly ground black pepper
- salt

1 Cook the spaghetti in salted boiling water until al dente and drain.

2 Transfer the pasta to a hot saucepan, sprinkle with half of the pecorino and add a grinding of pepper.

3 Season with salt and toss well. To serve, sprinkle with the remaining pecorino.

Linguine ai Calamaretti e carciofi

Linguine with squid and artichokes

Serves 4

- 12 ounces linguine
- 10 ounces squid
- 2 large artichokes, trimmed and peeled, chopped
- 2 cloves garlic, minced
- chopped parsley
- olive oil
- salt and freshly ground pepper

1 Clean the squid, removing the cartilage and ink sack.

2 In a deep skillet, sauté 1 clove of garlic and the parsley with 4 tablespoons of olive oil. When the garlic starts to brown, add the artichokes. Season with salt and pepper and cook over high heat, adding some water or fish stock.

3 In a separate skillet, sauté the remaining clove of garlic with 4 tablespoons of olive oil. Add the squid, season with salt and pepper and cook over high heat for about 5 minutes.

4 Cook to the pasta in salted boiling water until al dente. Drain and add to the squid. Toss well and add the artichokes.

5 Toss again and serve sprinkled with parsley.

Linguine con Calamaretti e salvia

Linguine with squid and sage

Serves 4

- 12 ounces linguine
- 10 ounces squid
- 2 cloves garlic
- 6 leaves fresh sage
- ½ cup white wine
- salt and freshly ground pepper
- olive oil

1 Clean the squid, removing the skin, the cartilage and ink sack. Cut into rings.

2 In a skillet, sauté the garlic and the sage in 6 tablespoons of olive oil. Add 1 tablespoon of water.

3 After a couple of minutes, add the squid rings, season with salt and pepper and sauté for a couple of minutes. Deglaze with the wine and cook for another 5 minutes.

4 Cook the pasta in salted boiling water until al dente. Add to the squid sauce and toss. Serve with a grinding of pepper.

Spaghetti alle Canocchie

Spaghetti with crayfish

Serves 4

- 12 ounces spaghetti or linguine
- 1 pound crayfish
- 2 cloves garlic
- chopped parsley
- 1/2 cup white wine
- olive oil
- minced chili pepper to taste
- salt

1 Cook the crayfish in 4 liters (4 quarts) of boiling salted water for about 5 minutes.

2 In a large deep skillet, warm 6 tablespoons of olive oil. Add the whole garlic, parsley and chili pepper and sauté.

3 When the garlic starts to brown, add the crayfish meat. Deglaze with the wine and cook until it evaporates. Season with salt and pepper and add some of the water where the crayfish was cooked.

4 Cook the pasta in the water where the crayfish was cooked until al dente. Drain and serve with the sauce.

Spaghetti alla Caprese

Spaghetti "Capri" style

Serves 4

- 12 ounces spaghettini (thin spaghetti)
- 14 ounces vine cherry tomatoes
- 6 ounces buffalo mozzarella
- minced chili pepper to taste
- 2 cloves garlic, minced
- chopped oregano
- salt
- olive oil

1 In a skillet, warm 6 tablespoons of olive oil. Add the garlic sliced in half, chili pepper and the tomatoes sliced in half. Season with salt and cook over high heat.

2 Cook the spaghettini in salted boiling water until al dente.

3 Drain and add to the skillet with the tomatoes. Toss well and add the mozzarella.

4 Remove from the heat and serve sprinkled with oregano.

Capellini alla *Caprese* con salsa cruda

Capellini with raw tomato sauce

Serves 4

- 12 ounces capellini or thin spaghettini
- 14 ounces peeled ripe tomatoes, seeds removed, chopped
- 8 ounces buffalo mozzarella, cubed
- 1 clove garlic, minced
- chopped basil
- olive oil
- salt and pepper

1 Blanch the tomatoes in boiling water and drain. Peel, remove the seeds and chop.

2 Transfer to a bowl and add the garlic sliced in half, some fresh basil, the mozzarella and 6 tablespoons of olive oil. Season with salt and pepper and set aside for about 30 minutes.

3 Cook the pasta in salted boiling water until al dente. Drain and add to the bowl. Toss and serve immediately.

Spaghetti alla Carbonara di verdure

Spaghetti with eggs and mixed vegetables

Serves 4

- 12 ounces spaghetti
- ½ onion
- 2 zucchini
- 1 bell pepper
- ½ eggplant
- 1 cabbage leaf
- 2 eggs
- salt and freshly ground pepper
- olive oil
- grated Parmigiano

1 Peel and dice the vegetables (you could choose others if desired). Sauté in a skillet over high heat with 6 tablespoons of olive oil, starting with the onion, then the bell pepper, eggplant, the cabbage and finally the zucchini.

2 Season with salt and pepper and cook for about 15 minutes.

3 Cook the pasta in salted boiling water until al dente. Drain and add to the skillet with the vegetables.

4 Add the eggs, season with salt and pepper and toss. Remove from the heat and serve with the Parmigiano on the side.

Spaghetti alla Carbonara

Spaghetti with eggs and pancetta

Serves 4

- 12 ounces spaghetti
- 1 whole egg, plus 2 yolks
- 4 ounces pancetta (cut into small thin slices)
- 1 clove garlic (optional)
- olive oil
- salt and pepper
- 2 tablespoons grated pecorino Romano
- 1/4 cup grated Parmigiano

1 In a large skillet, sauté the whole garlic in 3 tablespoons of olive oil. When it starts to brown, remove the garlic from the skillet and add the pancetta. Sauté over low heat until the fatty part is cooked but not crisp.

2 Cook the pasta in salted boiling water until al dente.

3 In a bowl, beat the egg with the yolks, 4 tablespoons of the combined cheeses. Season with salt and pepper and add 1 tablespoon of the water from the pasta.

4 Drain the pasta and add to the pancetta. Toss and cook for 1 minute.

5 Add to the bowl with the egg mixture and toss. Serve immediately with the remaining cheese and a grinding of pepper.

Linguine ai Carciofi

Linguine with artichokes

Serves 4

- 12 ounces linguine
- 4 small artichokes
- 2 cloves garlic, minced
- chopped parsley
- salt and freshly ground pepper
- olive oil
- grated Parmigiano

1 Peel the artichokes, removeing the outer leaves and the choke. Cut into pieces.

2 In a skillet, warm 6 tablespoons of olive oil. Add the garlic, artichokes and 5 tablespoons of water and cook over high heat for a couple of minutes.

3 Season with salt and pepper, add some more water if necessary and cover. Cover and cook over low heat until the artichokes are tender. At the end, add the parsley.

4 Cook the pasta in salted boiling water until al dente. Drain and add to the skillet with the artichokes. Toss and serve with the Parmigiano on the side.

Spaghetti al Cartoccio di mare

Spaghetti "en papillote"

Serves 4

- 12 ounces spaghetti or linguine
- 6 ounces squid
- 6 ounces shrimp
- 6 ounces clams
- 2 cloves garlic, minced
- chopped parsley
- minced chili pepper to taste
- ½ cup white wine
- olive oil
- salt

1 Clean the squid, removing the cartilage and ink sack. Cut into rings and set aside. Scrub the clams and place in a pot over high heat until open. Remove from the shells and set aside.

2 In large deep skillet, warm some olive oil. Add the garlic, chili pepper, parsley, squid and the unpeeled shrimp. Season with salt and cook for 5 minutes. Add the wine and cook until it starts to evaporate. Remove the shrimp, peel and return to the skillet along with the clams. Add more parsley and stir.

3 Cook the pasta in salted boiling water and drain just before it becomes al dente, reserving some of the cooking water. Add the pasta and the reserved water to the skillet with the seafood.

4 Place a large sheet of parchment paper or aluminum foil in a baking tray. Pour the pasta on the sheet and join the edges to close into a pouch, put into a preheated 400°F oven and bake for about 5 minutes. Serve immediately.

Bucatini al Cavolfiore

Bucatini with cauliflower

Serves 4

- 12 ounces bucatini
- 14 ounces cauliflower
- 14 ounces ripe peeled tomatoes, seeds removed, chopped
- 1 clove garlic, minced
- olive oil
- salt and freshly ground pepper
- grated Parmigiano or pecorino

1 Trim the cauliflower and boil for 15 minutes in salted water. Drain and divide into florets, discarding the tougher stems.

2 In a large skillet, sauté the garlic in 6 tablespoons of olive oil. Add the tomatoes, season with salt and pepper and cook over high heat for about 10 minutes.

3 Add the cauliflower florets and a bit of water and cook for about 5 minutes.

4 Cook the pasta in salted boiling water until al dente. Drain and add to the cauliflower. Serve with the cheese on the side.

Linguine con Cavolfiore uvetta e pinoli

Linguine with cauliflower, raisins, pinenuts

Serves 4

- 12 ounces linguine
- 14 ounces cauliflower
- 1 small onion
- 1/4 cup raisins soaked in water
- 1/4 cup pine nuts
- olive oil
- salt and freshly ground pepper
- grated Parmigiano (optional)

1 Trim the cauliflower and boil for 15 minutes in salted water. Divide into florets, discarding the tougher stems. Cut the florets into smaller pieces.

2 In a deep skillet, sauté the onion in 4 tablespoons of olive oil. Add the cauliflower, pine nuts, raisins and some of the cooking water from the cauliflower.

3 Season with salt and pepper and cook for about 10 minutes.

4 Cook the pasta in salted boiling water until al dente. Drain and transfer to a bowl with half of the cauliflower sauce. Serve with the remaining sauce on top. Add a grinding of pepper and serve the Parmigiano on the side if desired.

Spaghetti alla Checca o "picchi pacchiu"

Spaghetti with raw tomato sauce

Serves 4

- 12 ounces spaghetti
- 14 ounces San Marzano tomatoes or ripe cherry tomatoes
- 1 clove garlic, minced
- chopped basil
- olive oil
- salt

1 Prepare the sauce 1 hour before serving. Remove the seeds from the tomatoes (if necessary blanch shortly in boiling water and peel). Dice and place in a bowl.

2 Add 6 tablespoons of high quality olive oil, torn basil leaves, minced garlic, and season with salt and pepper. Set aside for 1 hour. Drain to remove the liquid that is given off.

3 Cook the pasta in salted boiling water until al dente. Drain and add to the bowl with the sauce. Toss and serve immediately.

Bucatini con Cime di rapa

Bucatini with turnip greens

Serves 4

- 12 ounces bucatini or thick spaghetti
- 1 pound turnip greens (top leaves)
- 2 anchovies packed in salt
- 2 cloves garlic, minced
- minced chili pepper to taste
- olive oil
- salt and freshly ground pepper
- grated pecorino

1 Clean, stem and wash the turnip leaves. Cook in salted boiling water for 20 minutes, drain and chop.

2 Meanwhile, in a skillet, warm 6 tablespoons of olive oil. Add the whole garlic, chili pepper and the anchovies and cook over high heat. Add the turnip greens to the skillet.

3 Cook the pasta in salted boiling water until al dente. Drain and add to the skillet and toss.

4 Serve, drizzled with olive oil. Finish with a grinding of pepper and the grated cheese.

Spaghetti alla Cipolla

Spaghetti with onions

Serves 4

- 12 ounces thick spaghetti or bucatini
- 2 large white onions (or 4 leeks)
- chopped thyme
- minced chili pepper to taste
- olive oil
- salt and freshly ground pepper
- grated Parmigiano or pecorino

1 Peel and thinly slice the onions and soak in cold water for about 1 hour.

2 In a deep skillet, warm 6 tablespoons of olive oil. Drain the onions and add to the skillet. Cook over low heat until soft and creamy yet not golden, stirring occasionally. Add thyme, chili pepper and season with salt.

3 Cook the pasta in salted boiling water until al dente. Drain and add to the onions. Serve with the grated cheese and finish with a grinding of pepper.

Spaghetti alle Cozze

Spaghetti with mussels

Serves 4

- 12 ounces spaghetti
- 1 1/2 pound mussels
- 14 ounces ripe peeled tomatoes, seeds removed, chopped
- 2 cloves garlic, minced
- chopped parsley
- minced chili pepper to taste
- salt
- olive oil

1 Scrub and debeard the mussels. Place in a pot over high heat until they open. Remove from the shell, reserving some in the shell for garnish and coarsely chop.

2 In a skillet, warm some olive oil. Add the garlic, parsley and chili pepper and sauté. When the garlic starts to brown, add the tomatoes and cook for about 20 minutes.

3 Add the mussels and the reserved cooking juices and cook for 5 minutes.

4 Cook the pasta in salted boiling water until al dente. Drain and add to the mussels. Sprinkle with chopped parsley and toss. Garnish with the reserved mussels in their shell.

Spaghetti con le Cozze all'ischitana

Spaghetti with mussels "Ischia" style

Serves 4

- 12 ounces spaghetti or linguine
- 1½ pound mussels
- 2 cloves garlic, minced
- chopped parsley
- olive oil
- salt and pepper

1 Scrub and debeard the mussels. Place in a pot over high heat until they open. Strain and reserve the liquid. Remove half the shell from the mussels.

2 In a large skillet, warm 8 tablespoons of olive oil. Add the garlic and parsley and sauté. When the garlic starts to brown, add the reserved juices from the mussels.

3 Add the mussels, season with salt and pepper and stir well.

4 Cook the pasta in salted boiling water until al dente. Drain and add to the skillet with the mussels. Toss and serve hot.

Spaghetti alle Erbe aromatiche

Spaghetti with aromatic herbs

Serves 4

- 12 ounces spaghetti or linguine
- 1 large white onion
- basil
- marjoram
- chives
- tarragon
- milk
- 4 tablespoons butter
- salt and pepper
- grated Parmigiano

1 In a food processor or with a knife, finely chop the leaves of the herbs.

2 In a deep skillet, melt the butter. Add the onion and sauté. When it starts to turn golden, add the herbs.

3 Season with salt and pour in the milk (or substitute heavy cream), stir and remove from the heat.

4 Cook the pasta in salted boiling water until al dente. Drain and transfer to a bowl. Pour the herb sauce over the pasta and toss. Finish with a grinding of pepper and serve with the Parmigiano on the side.

Spaghetti alla crema di Fiori di zucca

Spaghetti with squash blossom cream

Serves 4

- 12 ounces spaghetti or linguine
- 15 squash or zucchini blossoms, coarsely chopped
- 2 egg yolks
- 1 clove garlic
- 1 packet of saffron, dissolved in 1/4 cup of water
- 4 tablespoons butter
- salt and pepper
- grated Parmigiano

1 In a large skillet, melt the butter. Add the garlic and when it starts to brown, add the squash blossoms.

2 Sauté for a couple of minutes and add the saffron water.

3 Cook for 10 minutes and transfer to a food mill or food processor to puree. Return to the skillet. Season with salt and pepper and cook until the sauce reduces and turns creamy.

4 Cook the pasta in salted boiling water until al dente.

5 In a bowl, beat the egg yolks with 4 tablespoons of Parmigiano and 4 tablespoons of the water from the pasta.

6 Drain the pasta and add to the skillet with the sauce. Remove from the heat and pour in the yolk mixture. Stir well and serve with additional cheese.

Bucatini ai Fiori di zucca e zafferano

Bucatini with squash blossoms

Serves 4

- 12 ounces bucatini or spaghetti
- 20 squash or zucchini blossoms
- 5 ounces seeded peeled tomatoes, diced
- ½ white onion
- ½ teaspoon saffron
- olive oil
- salt and pepper
- grated Parmigiano

1 In a large skillet, warm 6 tablespoons of olive oil. Add the onion. When it starts to soften, add the squash blossoms.

2 Cook briefly and add the tomatoes. Season with salt and pepper and cook over high heat for about 5 minutes.

3 At the end add the saffron dissolved in a bit of boiling water.

4 Cook the pasta in salted boiling water until al dente. Drain and add to the sauce. Serve with the Parmigiano on the side.

Spaghetti in Frittata

Spaghetti frittata

Serves 4

- 6 ounces leftover spaghetti or linguine
- 2 eggs, beaten
- 1/4 cup milk
- 2 tablespoons butter
- salt and freshly ground pepper
- grated Parmigiano

1 Warm up the leftover pasta in boiling water. Drain, and transfer to a bowl.

2 Add the egg, 4 tablespoons of Parmigiano and the milk. Season with salt and pepper, and stir well.

3 In a skillet over medium heat, melt the butter. Pour in the egg mixture, cover, and cook for about 5 minutes.

4 When the frittata is set, and brown on the bottom, flip, and continue to cook on the other side. Serve with Parmigiano on the side.

Linguine ai Funghi porcini

Linguine with porcini mushrooms

Serves 4

- 12 ounces linguine
- 8 ounces fresh porcini mushrooms
- 6 ounces peeled ripe tomatoes, seeds removed, chopped
- 2 cloves garlic
- thyme or parsley
- olive oil
- salt and pepper

1 Peel the porcini and wash under running cold water. Finely dice.

2 In a deep skillet, warm 6 tablespoons of olive oil. Add the whole garlic and the herb.

3 When the garlic starts to brown, add the porcini and cook for about 5 minutes. Season with salt and pepper and add the tomatoes.

4 Cook, covered, over low heat for about 20 minutes. Remove and discard the garlic.

5 Cook the pasta in salted boiling water until al dente. Drain and transfer to a bowl. Pour the sauce over and toss.

Spaghetti alla *Gallinella* di mare

Spaghetti with snapper

Serves 4

- 12 ounces spaghetti or linguine
- 1 pound snapper
- 1 clove garlic
- chopped parsley
- olive oil
- salt and pepper

1 Clean the fish and boil in salted water for about 15 minutes.

2 Remove from the water and remove the meat from the bone. Transfer the meat to a food processor and grind.

3 In a skillet, warm 8 tablespoons of olive oil. Add the garlic and parsley and sauté. When the garlic starts to brown, add the fish meat and a bit of stock. Cook for a couple of minutes.

4 Cook the pasta in salted boiling water until al dente. Drain and add to the sauce. Season with salt and toss. Serve with a grinding of pepper.

Spaghetti con Gorgonzola e zucchini

Spaghetti with Gorgonzola and zucchini

Serves 4

- 12 ounces spaghetti or linguine
- 6 ounces sweet and creamy Gorgonzola
- 4 zucchini
- 2 tablespoons butter
- milk
- salt and white pepper
- olive oil
- grated Parmigiano

1 Trim the zucchini and slice into thin rounds. Sauté in a skillet with olive oil. Remove from the skillet and set aside to drain on paper towels.

2 In a saucepan, combine the milk with the butter and bring to a simmer. Crumble the gorgonzola into the saucepan. Season with salt and pepper and cook over low heat, stirring with a wooden spoon, until a smooth, creamy sauce forms.

3 Cook the pasta in salted boiling water until al dente, drain and add to the sauce.

4 Toss and stir in the zucchini. Serve with the Parmigiano.

Capellini al Gorgonzola

Capellini with Gorgonzola

Serves 4

- 12 ounces capellini or thin spaghetti
- 4 ounces sweet Gorgonzola
- 3 tablespoons butter
- ½ cup milk
- salt
- grated Parmigiano

1 Crumble the gorgonzola into a saucepan with the butter and milk. Season with salt and pepper and cook, stirring, over low heat for about 5 minutes.

2 Cook the pasta in salted boiling water until al dente. Drain and transfer to a bowl with a bit of the pasta water. Pour the gorgonzola sauce over the pasta.

3 Add 4 tablespoons of Parmigiano, toss and serve immediately, sprinkled with more cheese.

Spaghetti alla polpa di Granchio

Spaghetti with crab meat

Serves 4

- 12 ounces spaghetti
- 6 ounces crab meat
- 14 ounces peeled ripe tomatoes
- 1 clove garlic, minced
- 1 small bunch parsley, leaves only, chopped
- chili pepper
- salt
- olive oil

1 In a skillet, warm 6 tablespoons of olive oil. Add the garlic, parsley and chili pepper. When the garlic starts to brown, add the crab meat and cook for a couple of minutes.

2 Remove the crab meat mixture from the skillet and set aside. Add the tomatoes to the skillet, season with salt and cook over high heat for about 20 minutes.

3 Return the crab meat to the skillet and stir.

4 Cook the spaghetti in salted boiling water until al dente. Drain and add to the crab meat sauce along with extra parsley. Toss and serve.

Spaghetti ai Granchi

Spaghetti with crab

Serves 4

- 12 ounces spaghetti or linguine
- 8 blue crabs
- 1 pound ripe tomatoes
- 2 cloves garlic, minced
- 1/3 cup white wine
- chopped parsley
- minced chili pepper to taste
- olive oil
- salt

1 Boil the crabs in abundant salted water for about 5 minutes. Remove and on a cutting board, cut in half. Separate the body from the claws, without cracking.

2 In a skillet, warm 8 tablespoons of olive oil. Add the garlic and when it starts to brown, add the crab shell and claws and sauté for about 5 minutes. Deglaze with the wine and cook until it evaporates

3 Remove the crab from the skillet and with a fork, remove the meat from the shell and claws. Set the meat aside.

4 Add the tomatoes to the sauce in the skillet, add some parsley and the chili pepper. Season with salt and cook over high heat for about 15 minutes. At the end, add the crab meat.

5 Cook the pasta until al dente in the boiling water where the crabs were cooked. Drain and transfer to a pasta platter. Pour the crab sauce on top.

Spaghetti Mare e monti

Spaghetti "sea and mountain"

Serves 4

- 12 ounces spaghetti
- 1 pound clams
- 1 pound mussels
- 3 ounces fresh porcini mushrooms
- 6 ounces peeled ripe tomatoes, seeds removed, chopped
- 2 cloves garlic, minced
- chopped parsley
- 1/2 cup white wine
- salt and pepper
- olive oil

1 Scrub and debeard the mussels. Soak the clams in tempered water to rid the dirt.

2 Place the clams and mussels in a pot and cook over high heat until they open. Remove them from the pot and strain and reserve the cooking juice.

3 In a skillet, warm 6 tablespoons of olive oil. Add the garlic and parsley and sauté. When the garlic starts to brown, add the porcini. Cook for a couple of minutes and add the tomatoes. Season with salt and pepper and cook over high heat for about 10 minutes.

4 Add the clams and mussels and deglaze with the wine.

5 Cook the spaghetti in salted boiling water until al dente. Drain and add to the skillet with the mussels and clams. Toss to coat with the sauce and serve.

Linguine alle *Melanzane*

Linguine with eggplant

Serves 4

- 12 ounces linguine
- 2 small eggplants
- 8 ounces peeled ripe tomatoes, seeds removed, chopped
- 2 cloves garlic, minced
- chopped basil
- minced chili pepper to taste
- olive oil
- salt
- grated pecorino

1 Wash and cut the eggplant into cubes, without peeling.

2 In a deep skillet, warm 4 tablespoons of olive oil. Add the chili pepper, tomatoes and basil. Season with salt and cook over low heat.

3 In a separate skillet, warm 3 tablespoons of olive oil. Add the eggplant and cook over medium heat, stirring with a wooden spoon to prevent the eggplant from sticking to the skillet.

4 Cook the linguine in salted boiling water until al dente. Drain and combine in a bowl with the tomato sauce and the eggplant. Toss and serve with the grated cheese.

Spaghetti del Marinaio

Seaman's spaghetti

Serves 4

- 12 ounces spaghetti or linguine
- 6 ounces fresh anchovies
- 1 pound mussels
- 1 anchovy fillet packed in salt or oil
- 12 ounces peeled ripe tomatoes, seeds removed, chopped
- ½ onion
- 1 clove garlic, minced
- 1 tablespoon capers
- chopped parsley
- olive oil
- salt and pepper

1 Clean the fresh anchovies and remove the bones. Chop and set aside. Scrub and debeard the mussels. Place in a pot over high heat and cook until they open. Remove the mussels and strain and reserve the cooking juice.

2 In a skillet, warm 8 tablespoons of olive oil. Add the onion, garlic, parsley, capers, the anchovy fillet and chili pepper.

3 Cook for about 10 minutes. Deglaze with the wine and when it evaporates, add the tomatoes. Season with salt and cook for about 15 minutes.

4 Add the fresh anchovies and the mussels with their reserved cooking juice and cook for another 5 minutes. Toss in the parsley.

5 Cook the pasta in salted boiling water until al dente. Drain and add to the skillet. Toss and serve.

Spaghetti al Nero di seppia

Spaghetti with cuttlefish ink

Serves 4

- 12 ounces spaghetti or linguine
- 14 ounces cuttlefish with ink sack
- 2 ripe peeled tomatoes, seeds removed, chopped
- 2 cloves garlic, minced
- olive oil
- salt and pepper

1 Clean the cuttlefish, remove and discard the cartilage and remove and reserve the ink sack. Chop the cuttlefish into pieces.

2 In a skillet, warm 6 tablespoons of olive oil. Add the whole garlic and when it starts to brown, add the tomatoes and the chopped cuttlefish.

3 Season with salt and pepper and cook over low heat for about 20 minutes, stirring and adding hot water from time to time. At the end, stir in the ink from the ink sack.

4 Cook the pasta in salted boiling water until al dente. Drain and add to the skillet with the sauce. Toss and serve. Serve with a grinding of pepper.

Linguine alle Noci

Linguine with walnuts

Serves 4

- 12 ounces linguine or spaghetti
- 3 ounces shelled walnuts
- 2 slices white bread, crusts removed
- 1/2 clove garlic (optional)
- olive oil
- salt and pepper
- grated Parmigiano or pecorino (or both)

1 Blanch the walnuts in boiling water for a couple of minutes, drain and peel. Soak the bread in milk.

2 In a mortar or a food processor, finely grind the walnuts along with the soaked bread, garlic and a pinch of salt, until a pesto forms.

3 Transfer the pesto a bowl and stir in 4 tablespoons of grated cheese, a grinding of pepper and 1/4 cup of olive oil.

4 Cook the pasta in salted boiling water until al dente. Drain and combine in a bowl with the pesto and additional grated cheese. Toss and serve.

Spaghetti alla Norcina

Spaghetti with black truffles

86

Serves 4

- 12 ounces spaghetti
- 4 ounces black truffles
- 2 anchovy fillets packed in salt, rinsed
- olive oil
- salt and pepper

1 Rid the truffles of any dirt and mince or grind in a food processor until a paste forms.

2 In a skillet, warm 8 tablespoons of olive oil. Add the garlic, anchovies and 1 tablespoon of water.

3 Cook over low heat until the anchovies dissolve. Stir in the truffle paste and remove from the heat.

4 Cook the pasta in salted boiling water until al dente. Drain and add to a bowl. Pour the sauce over and toss.

5 Serve immediately and shave more truffles on top.

Spaghetti alla Norma

Spaghetti with eggplant "Norma" style

Serves 4

- 12 ounces spaghetti
- 2 medium eggplants
- 1 pound peeled ripe tomatoes, seeds removed, chopped
- 2 cloves garlic or 1/2 onion
- chopped basil
- olive oil
- salt and pepper
- grated ricotta salata

1 In a deep skillet, combine the garlic or onion with the tomatoes and 6 tablespoons of olive oil and season with salt and pepper.

2 Cook over high heat for about 15 minutes, add the basil and cook for another 15 minutes.

3 Meanwhile, slice the eggplant, without peeling and fry in olive oil until it starts to brown. Remove from the oil and set aside to drain in paper towels and keep warm.

4 Cook the pasta in salted boiling water until al dente. Drain and transfer to a bowl with the ricotta and the tomato sauce. Toss and serve sprinkled with more ricotta. Garnish with basil.

Linguine dell' Ortolano

Truck farmer's linguine

Serves 4

- 12 ounces linguine
- 14 ounces peeled ripe tomatoes, seeds removed, chopped
- 2 zucchini
- 1 small eggplant
- 1 yellow pepper
- 1 onion
- 1 carrot
- 1 stalk celery
- chopped basil
- olive oil
- salt and pepper
- grated Parmigiano

1 In a deep skillet, warm 6 tablespoons of olive oil. Add the onion and sauté until soft. At this point, add the vegetables.

2 Season with salt and pepper and cook for a couple of minutes. Add the tomatoes and basil and cook for about 30 minutes.

3 Cook the pasta in salted boiling water until al dente. Drain and add to a bowl. Pour the sauce over and serve with the Parmigiano on the side.

Bucatini alla Pastora

Shepherd's bucatini

Serves 4

- 12 ounces bucatini
- 14 ounces San Marzano tomatoes
- 1 clove garlic
- 1 ounce grated aged pecorino
- 1 ounce grated salted ricotta
- 1 ounce shredded spicy provolone
- olive oil
- salt and pepper

1 In a deep skillet, warm 6 tablespoons of olive oil. Add the garlic and when they start to brown, add the tomatoes. Season with salt and pepper and cook until it starts to reduce. Add half the pecorino, ricotta and provolone and stir well.

2 Cook the pasta in salted boiling water until al dente. Drain and add to the sauce. Add the remaining cheese and toss. Serve with a grinding of pepper.

Bucatini alla Pecorara

Bucatini with ricotta and sausage

Serves 4

- 12 ounces bucatini or thick spaghetti
- 10 ounces Italian pork sausage
- 6 ounces fresh sheep's milk ricotta
- bay leaves or fennel seeds
- salt and pepper
- olive oil
- grated pecorino

1 In a skillet, warm 3 tablespoons of olive oil. Remove the sausage from the casings and crumble into the skillet. Cook, stirring to break the sausage as much as possible.

2 Add a bay leaf or a pinch of fennel seeds and cook for a couple of minutes.

3 Cook the pasta in salted boiling water until al dente. Drain and transfer to a bowl with the ricotta. Season with salt and pepper and toss.

4 Add the sausage with its juices and toss. Serve with more ricotta and a grinding of pepper.

Linguine alla crema di Peperoni dolci

Linguine with sweet pepper cream

Serves 4

- 12 ounces linguine
- 2 large sweet yellow peppers
- 1 clove garlic
- chopped basil
- ½ cup milk or heavy cream
- 2 tablespoons butter
- olive oil
- salt and pepper
- grated Parmigiano

1 Wash the bell peppers. Remove and discard the seeds and inner white ribbing and chop.

2 In a skillet, warm 4 tablespoons of olive oil with the butter. Add the whole garlic and when it starts to brown, add the bell peppers. Season with salt and add a bit of water. Cook over low heat until the peppers are very tender.

3 Discard the garlic and transfer the peppers to a food processor. Puree until smooth.

4 Return the bell pepper puree to the skillet and add the milk or heavy cream and the basil. Season with salt and pepper and cook, stirring, until smooth and creamy.

5 Cook the pasta in salted boiling water until al dente. Drain and add, along with a bit of its cooking water, to the bell pepper cream. Toss and serve warm with the Parmigiano

Spaghetti ai Peperoni

Spaghetti with peppers

Serves 4

- 12 ounces thick spaghetti or linguine
- 8 ounces sweet yellow peppers
- 8 ounces peeled ripe tomatoes, seeds removed, chopped
- 1 onion
- chopped oregano or marjoram
- olive oil
- salt and pepper

1 Wash the peppers. Remove and discard the seeds and inner white ribbings. Cut into strips.

2 In a deep skillet, warm 6 tablespoons of olive oil. Add the onion and sauté until soft.

3 Add the peppers and tomatoes. Season with salt and cook uncovered for about 10 minutes. At the end, stir in the oregano or marjoram.

4 Cook the pasta in salted boiling water until al dente. Drain and add to the sauce. Toss and serve with a grinding of pepper.

Linguine con Peperoni e capperi

Linguine with peppers and capers

Serves 4

- 12 ounces linguine
- 9 ounces bell peppers
- 14 ounces peeled ripe tomatoes, seeds removed, chopped
- 2 cloves garlic
- 1 tablespoon capers packed in salt
- salt
- olive oil
- grated pecorino (optional)

1 Wash the pepper. Remove and discard the seeds and inner white ribbings. Place in a baking sheet and drizzle with olive oil. Place in a 350 degree oven until roasted. Peel and slice into strips.

2 In a skillet, warm 6 tablespoons of olive oil. Add the garlic and when it starts to brown, add the tomatoes. Cook for about 10 minutes and add the peppers. Stir and cover. Cook for about 10 minutes and add the capers, without rinsing.

3 Cook the pasta in salted boiling water until al dente. Drain and add to the sauce. Toss and serve with the pecorino on the side.

Spaghetti ai Peperoni e zafferano

Spaghetti with peppers and saffron

Serves 4

- 12 ounces spaghetti or bucatini
- 2 yellow bell peppers
- 1/4 cup pitted green olives
- 1 onion
- thyme
- 1 packet saffron
- olive oil
- salt and pepper
- grated Parmigiano

1 Remove and discard the seeds and inner white ribbing from the bell peppers. Cut into thin strips.

2 In a skillet, warm 6 tablespoons of olive oil. Thinly slice the onion, add to the skillet, and sauté until soft. Add the peppers, and cook over high heat until soft.

3 Slice the olives, and add to the skillet. Add some thyme, season with salt and pepper, and cook for another couple of minutes.

4 Soak the saffron in 1/4 cup of warm milk, and stir into the skillet.

5 Cook the pasta in salted boiling water until al dente. Drain the pasta, and add to the pepper mixture. Toss, and serve with Parmigiano on the side.

Spaghetti con il Pesce spada

Spaghetti with swordfish

Serves 4

- 12 ounces thick spaghetti or bucatini
- 8 ounces swordfish steak
- 2 cloves garlic, minced
- chopped parsley
- fennel seeds
- minced chili pepper to taste
- salt
- olive oil
- grated dried ricotta (optional)

1 Remove the skin from the swordfish and dice the meat.

2 In a skillet, warm 4 tablespoons of olive oil. Add the swordfish with the garlic, parsley, chili pepper and a pinch of crushed fennel seeds.

3 Season with salt and pepper and cook over high heat for about 5 minutes.

4 Cook the pasta in salted boiling water. Drain and add to the skillet with the swordfish. Toss and serve perhaps sprinkled with grated dried ricotta.

Bucatini con *Pesce spada* e melanzane

Bucatini with swordfish and eggplant

Serves 4

- 12 ounces bucatini or spaghetti
- 6 ounces swordfish steak
- 1 eggplant
- 1 clove garlic
- minced chopped oregano
- olive oil
- salt and pepper

1 In a skillet, warm 6 tablespoons of olive oil. Cut the eggplant, without peeling, into small cubes. Add to the skillet along with the 1 whole clove of garlic.

2 When it starts to brown, remove from the skillet and discard the garlic.

3 Cube the swordfish and add to the skillet with the other garlic clove and sauté.

4 Season with salt and pepper and add the oregano. Deglaze with wine or water and cook for about 15 minutes.

5 Cook the pasta in salted boiling water until al dente. Drain and add to the swordfish. Add the eggplant and toss. Serve immediately.

Trenette al Pesto genovese

Trenette with Genovese pesto

Serves 4

- 12 ounces trenette or linguine
- 1 cup fresh basil
- ½ clove garlic, minced
- 2 tablespoons pine nuts
- extra-virgin olive oil
- coarse salt
- grated Parmigiano and pecorino

1 Wash the basil leaves. Combine in a mortar with the garlic and a pinch of coarse salt.

2 With the pestle, press the ingredients against the walls of the mortar in a circular motion to grind them. When the basil is almost pasty, add the pine nuts and grind as well. This can alternatively be done in a food processor.

3 Transfer the pesto to a bowl and add 2 tablespoons each of Parmigiano and pecorino. Stir well, adding ½ cup of olive oil in a slow steady stream, until a dense sauce forms.

4 Cook the pasta in salted boiling water until al dente. Drain and transfer to a bowl. Add the pesto and toss. Serve sprinkled with extra cheese.

Linguine al Pesto e pomodorini

Linguine with pesto and tomatoes

Serves 4

- 12 ounces linguine
- 10 tablespoons pesto Genovese
- 1 pint cherry tomatoes
- 2 cloves garlic, minced basil
- salt and pepper
- olive oil

1 Prepare the pesto Genovese (recipe on page 100).

2 Wash and cut the tomatoes in half. Add to a skillet with 3 tablespoons of olive oil, and season with salt and pepper.

3 Cook over medium heat for about 10 minutes, stirring with a wooden spoon.

4 Cook the pasta in salted boiling water until al dente. Drain the pasta, and transfer to a bowl. Add 7 tablespoons of pesto Genovese, and toss.

5 To serve, transfer to a platter, top with the cherry tomatoes, and spoon the remaining 3 tablespoons of pesto on top.

Spaghetti al Pesto toscano

Spaghetti with Tuscan pesto

Serves 4

- 12 ounces spaghetti or linguine
- 3 ounces shelled, peeled walnuts
- 1 bunch basil, leaves only
- olive oil
- salt and pepper
- grated Parmigiano or pecorino

1 On a cutting board, mortar or food processor, mince or grind the basil and walnuts down to a paste.

2 Transfer to a bowl, season with salt and pepper and add 4 tablespoons of grated cheese.

3 Stir, adding olive oil in a slow, steady stream, until a creamy pesto sauce forms.

4 Cook the pasta in salted boiling water until al dente. Drain and transfer to a bowl with the pesto. Toss and serve sprinkled with more grated cheese.

Spaghetti al Pesto trapanese

Spaghetti with "Trapanese" pesto

Serves 4

- 12 ounces spaghetti or linguine
- 6 ounces ripe seeded and peeled tomatoes
- 2 ounces roasted peeled almonds
- 2 cloves garlic
- basil
- 2 ounces toasted bread crumbs
- olive oil
- salt and pepper

1 In a mortar, grind the almonds, garlic and basil down to a paste. Add the tomatoes and transfer to a bowl. Season with salt and pepper and add 6 tablespoons of olive oil in a slow, steady stream until a pesto-like sauce forms. This could alternatively be done in a food processor.

2 Cook the pasta in salted boiling water until al dente. Drain and transfer to a bowl. Add the pesto and toss.

3 Serve sprinkled with the toasted bread crumbs.

Spaghetti alla Pizzaiola

Spaghetti "pizza" style

Serves 4

- 12 ounces spaghetti
- 10 ounces peeled ripe tomatoes
- 5 ounces mozzarella, cubed
- basil
- oregano
- salt and pepper
- olive oil

1 In a deep skillet, combine the tomatoes with 3 tablespoons of olive oil and the basil and season with salt and pepper. Cook over high heat.

2 Cook the spaghetti in salted boiling water until al dente. Drain and add directly to the sauce.

3 Toss well and add the mozzarella, oregano, extra basil and a drizzle of olive oil.

4 When the mozzarella starts to melt, remove from the heat and serve immediately.

Spaghetti con le Polpettine "all'americana"

Spaghetti with meatballs

Serves 4

- 12 ounces spaghetti
- 12 ounces lean ground beef
- ½ onion
- 1 egg
- 1 bunch parsley, leaves only
- flour
- 2 cups tomato sauce
- basil
- salt and pepper
- olive oil
- grated Parmigiano

1 In a bowl, combine the beef with the onion, parsley and egg. Season with salt and pepper and work with your hands until it is well mixed.

2 Form the mixture into small meatballs. Dredge in flour and fry in a skillet with a little bit of oil for about 10 minutes, turning to cook on all sides.

3 Pour the tomato sauce (the recipe from the section dedicated to sauces) over the meatballs. Add the basil and cook over low heat for another 10 minutes.

4 Cook the spaghetti in salted boiling water until al dente. Drain and add to the meatball sauce. Sprinkle with Parmigiano and serve with more Parmigiano on the side.

Linguine con Polpo e zucchini

Linguine with octopus and zucchini

Serves 4

- 12 ounces linguine
- 1 pound octopus
- 9 ounces zucchini
- 2 cloves garlic, minced
- vegetable or fish stock
- chopped parsley
- salt and pepper
- olive oil

1 Cook the octopus in salted boiling water for about 30 minutes. Set aside to cool in the cooking water. Drain the octopus, and cut into small pieces.

2 In a skillet over low heat, warm 6 tablespoons of olive oil. Add the octopus and sauté, stirring, for about 10 minutes, adding some stock during the cooking.

3 Wash and thinly slice the zucchini. Add to the skillet, and season with salt and pepper. Cook over medium heat for another 10 minutes, adding stock during cooking if necessary.

4 Cook the pasta in salted boiling water until al dente. Drain the pasta, and add to the octopus sauce. Toss, and serve with a grinding of pepper.

Linguine ai Pomodori secchi

Linguine with sun dried tomatoes

Serves 4

- 12 ounces linguine or spaghetti
- 2 ounces sun dried tomatoes
- 10 ounces peeled ripe tomatoes
- 1 tablespoon capers packed in salt, rinsed
- 1 clove garlic
- chili pepper
- salt
- olive oil

1 Place the sun dried tomatoes in a skillet with 4 tablespoons of olive oil and 4 tablespoons of water and cook for about 5 minutes.

2 Add the peeled tomatoes and capers, the garlic and chili pepper. Season with salt and cook for 15 minutes.

3 Cook the linguine in salted boiling water until al dente. Drain and add to the sauce. Toss and serve. Cheese is optional.

Spaghetti ai Pomodori verdi

Spaghetti with green tomatoes

Serves 4

- 12 ounces spaghetti or linguine
- 1 pound bitter green tomatoes
- 2 cloves garlic
- basil
- salt and pepper
- olive oil

1 Wash and cut the tomatoes in half. Remove and discard the seeds and dice.

2 In a skillet over high heat, warm 6 tablespoons of olive oil. Add the garlic and tomatoes, and sauté for about 5 minutes.

3 Season with salt and pepper, and add some basil. Cook for another 5 minutes, and remove from the heat.

4 Cook the pasta in salted boiling water until al dente. Drain the pasta, and add to the tomato sauce. Serve immediately without cheese.

Spaghetti freddi al Pomodoro

Cold spaghetti with tomatoes

Serves 4

- 12 ounces spaghetti or thin spaghetti
- 12 ounces tomatoes
- 1 clove garlic, thinly sliced
- 5 ounces green or black olives, pitted and sliced
- basil, chopped
- chili pepper
- extra-virgin olive oil
- salt

1 Briefly blanch the tomatoes in boiling water. Drain, peel, remove the seeds and chop the tomatoes. Place in a bowl.

2 Add the garlic, olives, basil, chili pepper and season with salt.

3 Drizzle with 6 tablespoons of high quality olive oil, stir and set aside for about 30 minutes.

4 Cook the pasta in salted boiling water until al dente. Drain and transfer to a bath of ice water. Drain and add to the sauce. Toss and serve.

Linguine al Pomodoro e ricotta

Linguine with ricotta and tomatoes

Serves 4

- 12 ounces linguine
- 3 ounces fresh ricotta
- 8 ounces peeled ripe tomatoes, seeds removed, chopped
- chopped basil
- salt and pepper
- olive oil
- grated Parmigiano

1 In a skillet, warm 4 tablespoons of olive oil. Add the tomatoes, season with salt. Cook until it thickens, add the basil and remove from the heat.

2 Cook the pasta in salted boiling water until al dente. Drain and add to a bowl with the ricotta.

3 Pour the tomato sauce over the pasta and toss. Serve immediately with a grinding of pepper. The grated Parmigiano is optional.

Spaghettini al Pomodoro fresco

Spaghettini with fresh tomatoes

Serves 4

- 12 ounces spaghettini or linguine
- 1 pound San Marzano tomatoes
- 2 cloves garlic
- basil
- olive oil
- salt

1 Briefly blanch the tomatoes in boiling water. Drain, peel and remove the seeds. In a skillet, warm 6 tablespoons of olive oil. Add the whole garlic. Chop the tomatoes and add to the skillet. Season with salt and cook for 10 minutes.

2 When the sauce starts to reduce, add torn leaves of basil.

3 Cook the pasta in salted boiling water until al dente. Drain and add to the sauce. Toss and serve immediately.

Linguine con Prosciutto e piselli

Linguine with peas and ham

Serves 4

- 12 ounces linguine
- 5 ounces cooked ham, diced
- 6 ounces green peas
- 2 tablespoons butter
- 1/4 cup heavy cream
- 1 clove garlic, minced
- 1/2 teaspoon sugar
- olive oil
- grated Parmigiano

1 In a deep skillet, cook the peas with 1/2 cup of water, the whole garlic and 3 tablespoons of olive oil. Season with salt and the sugar.

2 In a separate skillet, melt the butter. Add the ham and cook for a couple of minutes. Add the pea mixture and stir.

3 Add the heavy cream, season with salt and pepper and cook over high heat.

4 Cook the pasta in salted boiling water until al dente. Drain and add to the sauce. Toss and serve with the Parmigiano on the side. As an alternative, add 3 oz of diced chicken breast to the ham.

Spaghetti al Profumo di mare

Fisherman's spaghetti

Serves 4

- 12 ounces spaghetti or linguine
- 8 ounces clams
- 8 ounces mussels
- 1 squid, cleaned and chopped
- 3 ounces shrimp
- 3 ripe peeled tomatoes, seeds removed, chopped
- 1 clove garlic, minced
- chopped parsley
- chopped basil
- olive oil
- salt and pepper

1 Scrub the clams. Scrub and debeard the mussels and combine in a pot with the clams. Cook over high heat until they open. Remove the clams and mussels and strain and reserve the cooking juice.

2 In a skillet, warm 8 tablespoons of olive oil. Mince the garlic, parsley and basil and add to the skillet. When the mixture starts to brown add the tomatoes.

3 Cook for a couple of minutes and add the squid and the shrimp.

4 Cook for 5 minutes and add the mussels and clams with the reserved cooking juices. Season with salt and pepper and cook over high heat for a couple of minutes.

5 Cook the pasta in salted boiling water until al dente. Drain and add to the skillet with the seafood. Toss and serve.

Spaghetti alla Puttanesca

Spaghetti "puttanesca"

Serves 4

- 12 ounces thin spaghetti or linguine
- 14 ounces peeled ripe tomatoes, seeds removed
- 4 anchovy fillets packed in salt, rinsed
- 3 ounces black olives, pitted and sliced
- 6 ounces small capers packed in salt, rinsed
- 2 cloves garlic, minced
- chopped parsley
- minced chili pepper to taste
- olive oil
- salt

1 In a large skillet, warm 6 tablespoons of olive oil. Add the garlic and sauté. When it starts to brown, add the chili pepper and the anchovies and stir.

2 Remove the garlic and add the tomatoes, capers and olives.

3 Season with salt if necessary and cook over high heat for about 15 minutes. At the end, sprinkle the sauce with parsley.

4 Cook the pasta in salted boiling water until al dente. Drain and add to the sauce. Toss and serve, sprinkled with more parsley.

Spaghetti al Radicchio rosso

Spaghetti with red radicchio

Serves 4

- 12 ounces spaghetti
- 14 ounces red radicchio (trimmed and shred)
- 3 ounces fontina cheese (or Emmental), cubed
- ½ onion
- ground nutmeg
- milk
- salt and pepper
- olive oil

1 In a skillet, warm 4 tablespoons of olive oil and add the onion. When it starts to brown, add the radicchio.

2 Cook, covered, over medium heat. When the radicchio is tender, season with salt, pepper and a pinch of nutmeg. Add a splash of milk and cook for 5 minutes.

3 Cook the spaghetti in salted boiling water until al dente. Drain and add to the skillet with the sauce. Add the fontina and toss. Serve with a grinding of pepper.

Spaghetti alla Rucola

Spaghetti with arugula

Serves 4

- 12 ounces spaghetti or linguine
- 3 ounces arugula
- 1 clove garlic
- minced chili pepper to taste
- 2 anchovy fillets (optional)
- salt
- olive oil
- grated pecorino

1 Wash the arugula, dry well and chop. Cook the pasta in salted boiling water until al dente.

2 Meanwhile in a skillet, warm 6 tablespoons of olive oil. Add the garlic, chili pepper and anchovies. Add 2 tablespoons of water.

3 Cook slowly so that the garlic doesn't brown. Drain the pasta and add to the skillet with the sauce along with the arugula.

4 Toss and serve with the pecorino on the side.

Bucatini alla Ricotta

Bucatini with ricotta

Serves 4

- 12 ounces bucatini or thick spaghetti
- 3 ounces ricotta
- 4 tablespoons fresh pecorino or sweet provolone shredded
- 4 tablespoons butter, diced
- salt and pepper
- grated pecorino and Parmigiano

1 In a bowl, combine the ricotta with the fresh pecorino or sweet provolone and the butter. Season with salt and pepper and mix well. Keep warm in the oven.

2 Cook the pasta in salted boiling water until al dente. Drain, reserving 1/2 cup of the cooking water.

3 Transfer the pasta to the bowl with the ricotta. Toss, adding the reserved water from the pasta, until a creamy sauce forms. Serve with a grinding of pepper. The grated Parmigiano or pecorino is optional.

Bucatini con le Sarde

Bucatini with sardines

Serves 4

- 12 ounces bucatini
- 14 ounces fresh sardines
- 3 ounces wild fennel
- ½ onion, chopped
- 2 anchovy fillets packed in salt, rinsed
- 2 tablespoons pine nuts
- 1 tablespoon raisins soaked in water
- pinch of saffron
- olive oil
- salt and pepper

1 Clean the sardines and remove the bones.

2 Trim the wild fennel and boil in salted water for 15 minutes. Drain, reserving the cooking water and finely chop.

3 In a skillet, warm 6 tablespoons of olive oil. Add the onion and the anchovies and sauté. When the onion is soft, add the sardine fillets and cook on all sides. Remove the sardines from the skillet and keep warm. Add the wild fennel, pine nuts and raisins to the skillet and season with salt and pepper.

4 Dissolve the saffron in a bit of the water reserved from the wild fennel. Add to the skillet, cover and cook for about 10 minutes.

5 Cook the pasta in the remaining water from the wild fennel until al dente. Drain and combine in a bowl with the sauce and the sardines.

Bucatini con Sarde e cavolfiore

Bucatini with sardines and cauliflower

Serves 4

- 12 ounces bucatini
- 14 ounces cauliflower, trimmed
- 4 fresh sardines
- ½ onion, chopped
- 1 clove garlic
- 1 tablespoon pine nuts
- 1 tablespoon raisins soaked in water
- pinch of saffron
- minced chili pepper to taste
- ½ cup white wine
- olive oil
- salt

1 Cook the cauliflower in boiling water until tender. Remove from the water and divide into florets.

2 Clean the sardines and remove the bones.

3 In a skillet, warm 6 tablespoons of olive oil. Add the onion, garlic and chili pepper and cook until the onion starts to brown. Add the pine nuts and raisins and cook for a couple of minutes. Add the cauliflower florets, the wine and saffron and season with salt and pepper.

4 Cook, stirring, for 5 minutes, adding some water if necessary. At this point add the sardine and cook for about 5 minutes.

5 Cook the pasta in salted boiling water until al dente. Drain and add to the sauce. Toss and serve. This pasta is just as good eaten cold.

Spaghetti con Scampi alla bùsara

Spaghetti with scampi "Bùsara" style

Serves 4

- 12 ounces spaghetti
- 14 ounces scampi (or large shrimp)
- 14 ounces ripe peeled tomatoes, chopped
- 1 clove garlic, minced
- chopped parsley
- 1/4 cup Brandy or Cognac
- flour
- minced chili pepper to taste
- olive oil
- salt

1 Peel, butterfly and devein the scampi (or shrimp).

2 In a skillet sauté the garlic, parsley and chili pepper in olive oil. When the garlic starts to brown, add the scampi.

3 Sauté for about 3 minutes, deglaze with the Brandy and cook over high heat until it evaporates. Sprinkle with flour.

4 Add the tomatoes, season with salt and cook for 15 minutes. At the end sprinkle with extra chopped parsley and a drizzle of olive oil.

5 Cook the pasta in salted boiling water until al dente. Drain and toss with the scampi sauce.

Linguine agli Scampi

Linguine with scampi

Serves 4

- 12 ounces linguine or spaghetti
- 14 ounces scampi (or medium shrimp)
- 2 cloves garlic, minced
- chopped parsley
- minced chili pepper to taste
- 1/2 cup white wine
- salt
- olive oil

1 Wash the prawns and cut in half lengthwise. In a skillet, warm 6 tablespoons of olive oil. Add the whole garlic, parsley, chili pepper and prawns.

2 Cook briefly, season with salt and deglaze with the wine.

3 Cook until the wine evaporates, and cover the skillet.

4 Cook the pasta in salted boiling water until al dente. Drain and add to the skillet with the prawns. If desired, peel the prawns before adding the pasta.

Spaghetti allo Scoglio

Spaghetti "Rocks" style

Serves 4

- 12 ounces spaghetti
- 8 ounces mussels, scrubbed and debearded
- 8 ounces clams, scrubbed
- 4 ounces shrimp
- 3 ounces squid
- 8 ounces peeled ripe tomatoes (optional)
- 2 cloves garlic
- chopped parsley
- minced chili pepper to taste
- olive oil
- salt

1 Place the mussels and clams in a pot over high heat and cook until they open. Drain and reserve the strained cooking juice. Peel the shrimp. Clean the squid, removing the cartilage and ink sack and cut into rings.

2 In a skillet, warm 8 tablespoons of olive oil. Add the garlic, chili pepper and parsley.

3 When the garlic starts to brown, add the reserved cooking juices from the mussels and clams and the tomatoes. Season with salt and cook over high heat for about 10 minutes.

4 At this point, add the clams, mussels, squid and shrimp and some more parsley and cook for another 10 minutes.

5 Cook the pasta in salted boiling water until al dente. Drain and add to the sauce with the seafood. Toss and serve.

Linguine allo Scorfano

Linguine with scorpion fish

Serves 4

- 12 ounces linguine or spaghetti
- 10 ounces red scorpion (rock) fish fillet, skin removed
- 1 pound ripe tomatoes
- 2 cloves garlic, minced
- chopped parsley
- minced chili pepper to taste
- ½ cup white wine
- olive oil
- salt

1 In a skillet, warm 6 tablespoons of olive oil. Add 1 garlic clove, the parsley and chili pepper and sauté. When the garlic starts to brown, add the scorpion fish fillet.

2 Cook for a couple of minutes, deglaze with the wine and cook until it evaporates. Remove the fish from the skillet and set aside.

3 Add the tomatoes to the skillet. Season with salt and cook for about 30 minutes. Add water or fish stock if it becomes to dry.

4 Divide the scorpion fish into pieces and add to the sauce along with more parsley and 2 tablespoons of olive oil.

5 Cook the pasta in salted boiling water until al dente. Drain and add directly to the skillet with the sauce. Toss and serve.

Spaghetti alle Seppie

Spaghetti with cuttlefish

130

Serves 4

- 12 ounces spaghetti or linguine
- 1 pound cuttlefish
- 2 peeled ripe tomatoes, seeds removed, chopped
- 2 cloves garlic, minced
- olive oil
- grated pecorino (optional)

1 Clean the cuttlefish, removing the cartilage. Remove and reserve the ink sack. Chop the cuttlefish.

2 In a skillet, warm 6 tablespoons of olive oil. Add the onion and garlic and sauté. When they start to brown, add the tomatoes and the cuttlefish.

3 Season with salt and pepper and cook, stirring occasionally, for about 30 minutes. At the end, stir in the ink from the ink sack, add a bit of water or stock if necessary and cook for another 15 minutes.

4 Cook the pasta in salted boiling water until al dente. Drain and add to the sauce. Toss and serve. The grated pecorino is optional.

Spaghetti alla Siracusana

Spaghetti "Siracusa"

Serves 4

- 12 ounces spaghetti
- 14 ounces peeled ripe tomatoes, seeds removed, chopped
- 2 ounces green or black olives, pitted and sliced
- 1 sweet yellow pepper
- 1 eggplant
- 2 fresh anchovies, cleaned and debunked
- 1 clove garlic, minced
- 1 tablespoon capers packed in salt, rinsed
- chopped basil
- olive oil
- salt and pepper
- grated pecorino or caciocavallo

1 Remove and discard the seeds and inner white ribbing from the sweet yellow pepper and julienne. Cut the eggplant into small cubes and remove the seeds from the tomatoes.

2 In a skillet, warm 6 tablespoons of olive oil. Add the garlic, pepper, eggplant and anchovies.

3 When the vegetables starts to brown, add the tomatoes, capers and olives. Adjust seasonings and cook for about 20 minutes. At the end, add the basil.

4 Cook the pasta in salted boiling water until al dente. Drain and add to the sauce. Toss and serve with the grated cheese.

Spaghetti alla Sorrentina

Spaghetti "Sorrento"

Serves 4

- 12 ounces thin spaghetti
- 14 ounces peeled ripe tomatoes, seeds removed, diced
- 3 ounces green Gaeta olives, pitted and quartered
- 6 anchovy fillets
- 1 tablespoon capers packed in salt
- 1 clove garlic, minced
- chopped parsley
- minced chili pepper to taste
- salt
- olive oil

1 In a skillet, warm 4 tablespoons of olive oil. Add the olives, anchovies, capers, chili pepper and garlic.

2 Cook over low heat for a couple of minutes and add the tomatoes. Cover and cook for about 30 minutes.

3 Cook the spaghettini in salted boiling water until al dente. Drain and add to the sauce.

4 This preparation is just as good without the tomatoes. In this case, add 3 tablespoons of water to the olive and anchovies after cooking.

Linguine alla *Spigola*

Linguine with sea bass

Serves 4

- 12 ounces linguine or spaghetti
- 1 small sea bass (around 1 pound)
- 2 cloves garlic, minced
- chopped parsley
- minced chili pepper to taste
- ½ cup white wine
- olive oil
- salt

1 In a skillet, warm 6 tablespoons of olive oil. Add 1 clove of garlic, the parsley and chili pepper.

2 When the garlic starts to brown, add the fish. Season with salt and deglaze with the wine.

3 Cook for 15 minutes and remove the fish. Break into pieces and return to the skillet.

4 Cook the pasta in salted boiling water until al dente. Drain and add to the fish sauce. Toss and serve.

Linguine con il *Tonno* alla siciliana

Linguine with tuna "Sicilian" style

Serves 4

- 12 ounces linguine or spaghetti
- 3 ounces canned tuna packed in oil, drained
- 2 ounces black olives, pitted
- 1 tablespoon capers packed in salt
- 1 clove garlic, minced
- chopped parsley
- olive oil
- salt and pepper

1 In a skillet, warm 6 tablespoons of olive oil. Add the garlic, parsley, olives and capers and sauté for a couple of minutes.

2 Shred the tuna into the skillet and add a couple of tablespoons of water and a grinding of pepper. Cook over low heat for about 5 minutes.

3 Cook the pasta in salted boiling water until al dente. Drain and add to the sauce. Toss and serve sprinkled with parsley.

Spaghetti al ragù di Tonno fresco

Spaghetti with fresh tuna sauce

Serves 4

- 12 ounces spaghetti
- 8 ounces fresh tuna steak
- 12 ounces peeled ripe tomatoes, seeds removed, chopped
- 2 cloves garlic
- chopped parsley
- olive oil
- salt and pepper

1 In a skillet warm 4 tablespoons of olive oil. Add the tuna fillet and sauté on both sides very shortly (tuna steak should be rare). Remove from the skillet and discard the oil. Remove the skin from the tuna and cut the fillet into small cubes.

2 In a skillet warm 6 tablespoons of olive oil and add the whole garlic. When it starts to brown, add the tomatoes. Season with salt and pepper and cook for about 15 minutes.

3 Add the cubed tuna fillet and the parsley and cook for another 2 minutes.

4 Cook the pasta in salted boiling water until al dente. Drain and transfer to a bowl. Pour the ragù on top and serve.

Spaghetti al Tonno sott'olio

Spaghetti with tuna

Serves 4

- 12 ounces spaghetti
- 3 ounces tuna packed in oil, drained
- 1 anchovy fillet packed in oil, drained
- 14 ounces peeled ripe tomatoes, seeds removed, chopped
- 1 clove garlic, minced
- chopped parsley
- chopped oregano
- olive oil
- salt and pepper

1 In a skillet, warm 6 tablespoons of olive oil. Add the garlic and parsley and sauté briefly. Add the anchovy, season with salt and cook over low heat.

2 Add the tomatoes, season with salt and pepper and cook for about 20 minutes until the sauce starts to thicken.

3 At the end, add the tuna, a pinch of oregano and more parsley.

4 Cook the pasta in salted boiling water until al dente. Drain and transfer to a bowl. Pour the tuna sauce on top and serve.

Linguine alle Triglie

Linguine with mullet

Serves 4

- 12 ounces linguine or spaghetti
- whole medium red mullet, about 14 ounces (scaled and cleaned)
- 2 cloves garlic, minced
- chopped parsley
- minced chili pepper to taste
- ½ cup white wine
- olive oil
- salt

1 In a skillet, warm 6 tablespoons of olive oil. Add the garlic, parsley and chili pepper and sauté. When the garlic starts to brown, add the mullet and cook for 2 minutes. Deglaze with wine.

2 Season with salt and cook for about 5 minutes, without turning. When the meat starts to fall apart, remove from the skillet and carefully shred.

3 Return the fish to the skillet with the garlic and parsley and bring to a simmer. Cook the pasta in salted boiling water until al dente. Drain, reserving some of the cooking water and add the pasta to the skillet.

4 Stir over the heat, adding the reserved water from the pasta. Cook until it starts to thicken and becomes almost creamy.

Linguine alla Trabaccolara

Linguine with mixed fish sauce

Serves 4

- 12 ounces linguine or spaghetti
- 1 pound whole fish, cleaned, deboned and skin removed
- 6 ounces peeled ripe tomatoes, seeds removed, chopped
- 1 clove garlic, minced
- chopped parsley
- minced chili pepper to taste
- 1/2 cup white wine
- olive oil
- salt

1 In a skillet, warm 6 tablespoons of olive oil. Add the garlic, parsley and chili pepper and sauté. When the garlic starts to brown, add the fish and cook for about 10 minutes, degassing with the wine.

2 Remove the skillet from the heat, remove the fish from the skillet and shred the fish meat to pieces. Return the fish to the skillet with the garlic and parsley and add the tomatoes.

3 Season with salt and cook, uncovered, for 15 minutes. Add parsley and remove from the heat.

4 Cook the pasta in salted boiling water until al dente. Drain and add to the sauce. Toss and serve.

Spaghetti appetitosi alle Verdure

Spaghetti with vegetables

Serves 4

- 12 ounces spaghetti or linguine
- 14 ounces peeled ripe tomatoes
- 2 ounces pitted black olives
- 1 yellow bell pepper, seeds and inner white ribbing removed, julienned
- 1 eggplant, unpeeled, cubed
- 1 tablespoon capers
- 1 clove garlic
- 2 anchovy fillets packed in oil or salt, rinsed
- chopped basil
- minced chili pepper to taste
- salt
- olive oil

1 In a skillet warm 6 tablespoons of olive oil. Add the garlic and chili pepper and sauté. When they start to brown, add the tomatoes and cook over high heat for about 15 minutes.

2 Add the eggplant and the yellow bell pepper and cook for another 10 minutes. Add the olives, capers, anchovy fillets and basil.

3 Season with salt and cook over high heat for another 5 minutes.

4 Cook the pasta in salted boiling water until al dente. Drain and add to the sauce. Toss and serve.

Spaghetti al Vino rosso

Spaghetti with red wine sauce

Serves 4

- 12 ounces thick spaghetti
- 3 ounces pancetta
- ½ onion
- 1 cup full-bodied red wine
- salt and pepper
- olive oil
- grated Parmigiano or pecorino

1 Finely chop the onion, and cut the pancetta into fine dice.

2 In a skillet over medium heat, warm 4 tablespoons of olive oil. Add the onion and pancetta, and sauté. When the onion starts to soften, season with salt and pepper. Deglaze with ½ cup of red wine, and cook until it evaporates.

3 Cook the pasta in salted boiling water, to which ½ cup of red wine has been added, until al dente. Drain the pasta, and add to the skillet.

4 Add a splash of red wine, and toss over high heat.

5 Serve with a grinding of fresh pepper and grated aged cheese.

Spaghetti alle Vongole

Spaghetti with clams and tomatoes

Serves 4

- 12 ounces spaghetti or linguine
- 1½ pounds clams
- 8 ounces peeled ripe tomatoes, seeds removed, chopped
- 1 clove garlic, minced
- chopped parsley
- minced chili pepper to taste
- olive oil
- salt

1 Scrub the clams. Place in a pot over high heat and cook until they open. Remove the clams and strain and reserve the cooking juices.

2 In a skillet, warm 6 tablespoons of olive oil. Add the garlic, parsley and chili pepper. When the garlic starts to brown, pour in the reserved cooking juices from the clams and cook until it starts to reduce. Add the tomatoes, season with salt and cook for about 15 minutes.

3 Add the clams and more parsley, bring to a boil and remove from the heat.

4 Cook the pasta in salted boiling water until al dente. Drain and transfer to a bowl. Pour the sauce over and serve.

Spaghetti alle Vongole in bianco

Spaghetti with white clam sauce

Serves 4

- 12 ounces spaghettini or linguine
- 2 pounds clams
- 1 clove garlic, minced
- chopped parsley
- minced chili pepper to taste
- ½ cup white wine
- olive oil
- salt

1 Scrub the clams and place in a pot. Cook over high heat until they open. Remove the clams and strain and reserve the leftover juice.

2 In a skillet, warm 8 tablespoons of garlic. Add the garlic, parsley and chili pepper. When the garlic starts to brow, deglaze with the wine and cook until it evaporates.

3 Add the clams, the strained leftover juices and some more parsley. Season with salt and cook for a couple of minutes.

4 Cook the pasta in salted boiling water until al dente. Drain and add to the clam sauce. Add some of the cooking water from the pasta if necessary, toss and serve.

Linguine alle Vongole e zucchini

Linguine with clams and zucchini

Serves 4

- 12 ounces linguine or spaghetti
- 1½ pounds clams
- 8 ounces zucchini, sliced
- 1 clove garlic, minced
- chopped parsley
- minced chili pepper to taste
- olive oil
- salt and pepper

1 Place the clams in a pot and cook over high heat until they open. Remove from the shells (or leave on) and strain and reserve the cooking juices.

2 In a skillet, warm 6 tablespoons of olive oil. Add the garlic, parsley and chili pepper. When the garlic starts to brown, add the zucchini.

3 Season with salt and cook over high heat for 10 minutes. Add the clams and their reserved cooking juices.

4 Cook the pasta in salted boiling water until al dente. Drain and add to the skillet. Sprinkle with more parsley, toss and serve.

Spaghetti con Zucca e gamberetti

Spaghetti with pumpkin and shrimp

Serves 4

- 12 ounces spaghetti or linguine
- 10 ounces pumpkin
- 6 ounces shrimp
- 1/2 white onion
- minced chili pepper to taste
- chopped parsley
- 1/2 cup white wine
- olive oil
- salt and pepper

1 Peel the pumpkin and remove the seeds. cut into fine dice.

2 Finely chop the onion and sauté along with the chili pepper in a skillet with 4 tablespoons of olive oil. Add the pumpkin and cook for about 5 minutes.

3 Peel the shrimp and add to the skillet. Deglaze with the wine, season with salt and pepper and cook over high heat until the wine starts to evaporate.

4 Cook the pasta in salted boiling water until al dente. Drain and add to the skillet. Toss and serve sprinkled with parsley. If desired, it can be served sprinkled with grated Parmigiano.

Linguine con la Zucca

Linguine with pumpkin

Serves 4

- 12 ounces linguine
- 1 pound pumpkin
- 6 ounces peeled ripe tomatoes, seeds removed, chopped
- ½ onion
- milk
- salt and freshly ground pepper
- olive oil
- Parmigiano

1 In a skillet, warm 4 tablespoons of olive oil. Add the onion and sauté. Peel the pumpkin, remove the seeds and dice the pulp. Add to the skillet and sauté.

2 After 5 minutes, add the tomatoes and cook over low heat for about 15 minutes. Season with salt and pepper.

3 Cook the linguine in salted boiling water until al dente. Drain and add to the skillet with the pumpkin.

4 Add some milk and some Parmigiano Toss and serve with a grinding of pepper.

Bucatini agli Zucchini

Bucatini with zucchini

Serves 4

- 12 ounces bucatini or spaghetti
- 1 pound small zucchini
- 1 clove garlic
- olive oil
- salt and pepper
- 2 ounces sweet provolone
- 2 ounces grated Parmigiano

1 In a skillet, warm 6 tablespoons of olive oil. Wash and slice the zucchini into 1/2-inch pieces and add to the skillet along with the garlic.

2 Cook over high heat, without burning, until tender. Remove with a slotted spoon and set aside to drain on paper towels.

3 Cook the pasta in salted boiling water until al dente. Drain and add to the skillet where the zucchini was cooked. Add the zucchini and half the Parmigiano. Season with pepper, toss and serve sprinkled with the remaining Parmigiano.

Recipe index

Ingredient index

Paolo Petroni is a native of Florence, where he's head of a marketing Agency. His books are known and appreciated throughout Italy as well as in the United States. The clarity and simplicity of the recipes are the force behind his publications.

Each of the recipes is carefully designed and tested in order to ensure success, eliminating long and superfluous procedures.

Paolo Petroni is a journalist, editor in chief of a famous Restaurant Guide and an avid wine enthusiast and gourmand. He is honorary delegate of the Florence chapter and a councilor of the Italian Academy of Cuisine (Accademia Italiana della Cucina).

Other books from the author

Il libro della vera cucina fiorentina

Il libro della vera cucina marinara

Il grande libro della vera cucina toscana

Il libro della vera cucina emiliana e romagnola

Il libro della pasta e del riso

Spaghetti amore mio

The complete book of Florentine cooking